Praise for
*God of the Fairy Tale*

"There is Truth woven into the fabric of fairy tales (as indeed there is in all creation). Jim Ware has thoughtfully begun to unravel that Truth. He has listened and heard the echoes of it as they have reverberated throughout the classic children's stories we all love and thought we knew. He has drawn from his belt the golden goblet and poured the magic, eye-opening potion in our left eye so that, in time, we will begin to see not simply with but *through* them."

—MICHAEL CARD, author of *A Fragile Stone* and *Scribbling in the Sand*

"Truth has always been found in the most unlikely of places. What a fresh, enlightening perspective to the exercise of seeking out the God of the upside-down kingdom! This is a rare look into the magic mirror, a new twist on who the fairest truly is, and a chance to be awed and inspired by the man behind the curtain."

—DAN HASELTINE, songwriter, jars of clay

"*God of the Fairy Tale* is a beautifully written book that treats stories not as an academic exercise but as God-given mysteries to explore. It's a warm, poetic devotional that turns our eyes to God and allows us to find Him in unlikely places and through unlikely characters. Jim is a remarkable worker of words and stories. Families of all ages can make great use of this marvelous book."

—PAUL McCUSKER, author of *Epiphany* and the Adventures in Odyssey Passages series

"*God of the Fairy Tale* is a brilliant blend of art and inspiration from a truly gifted writer. Be prepared to recapture the magic of your faith!"

—KURT BRUNER, coauthor of *Finding God in the Lord of the Rings*

"This is not a safe book! But it is a very good book. It will open your mind to the great truths behind the classic stories you enjoyed in your youth. Plus it will enrich your family as you reread these stories with your children."

—AL JANSSEN, author of *The Marriage Masterpiece*

"In Ware's handling, the classic fairy stories emerge as what C. S. Lewis called good dreams that God sent to the human race— imaginary stories and myths that are analogous to patterns that we find in the Bible and the Christian faith. For Christian readers and parents who have not known what to make of fairy tales, this book provides helpful answers as it sets up a two-way street in which the Christian faith and the genre of the fairy tale reveal the truth and beauty of each other."

—DR. LELAND RYKEN, professor of English at Wheaton College and author of more than two dozen books, including *The Christian Imagination: The Practice of Faith in Literature and Writing*

"Jim Ware offers a compelling explanation of not only how literature transforms the soul, but how traditional stories, myths, and fairy tales have 'come true' in Christ! Especially helpful for the 'literature-challenged.'"

—HANK HANEGRAAFF, host of the *Bible Answer Man* radio broadcast

# JIM WARE

# GOD
## OF
## THE
# FAIRY TALE

FINDING TRUTH IN THE LAND *of* MAKE-BELIEVE

SHAW BOOKS
*an imprint of* WATERBROOK PRESS

*God of the Fairy Tale*
A SHAW BOOK
PUBLISHED BY WATERBROOK PRESS
2375 Telstar Drive, Suite 160
Colorado Springs, Colorado 80920
*A division of Random House, Inc.*

ISBN 0-87788-049-2

Published in association with the literary agency of Alive Communications, Inc., 7680 Goddard Street, Suite 200, Colorado Springs, CO 80920.

Library of Congress Cataloging-in-Publication Data
Ware, Jim.
    God of the fairy tale : finding truth in the land of make-believe / Jim Ware—1st ed.
        p. cm.
    Includes bibliographical references.
    ISBN 0-87788-049-2
    1. Fairy tales—History and criticism.  2. Fairy tales—Religious aspects.  I. Title.
    PN3437.W37
    2003 398.2—dc21

                                        2003011252

Printed in the United States of America
2003—First Edition

10 9 8 7 6 5 4 3 2 1

# Contents

*To Kurt, for his encouragement,
and to Ken, who helped make it possible*

Prologue

# A Tree by Another Name

*Finding God in Fairy Tales*

*I suspect that men have sometimes derived more
spiritual sustenance from myths they did not believe
than from the religion they professed.*
—C. S. Lewis

*True? This very thing I have been telling you
is the truest I could dish out for you, my friends,
and belongs to my life too, in a certain sense.*
—E. T. A. Hoffman, "The Golden Flowerpot"

September 1931. *A dark and stormy night.* Windy, at any rate. On the grounds of Magdalen College, Oxford, two tweed-jacketed, pipe-puffing professors go crunching down the gravel path known as Addison's Walk under the deeper shadows of an ancient grove of trees—a mysterious, murky wood where, in the blustery darkness, it's easy to imagine elves among the branches.

"Look!" says the tall, long-faced fellow with the furrowed

brow and twinkling eyes of a sage...or a wizard. "There it stands—its feet in the earth, its head among the stars. A majestic miracle of creation! And what do we call it? A *tree*." He laughs. "The word falls absurdly short of expressing the thing itself."

"Of course it does," responds the other, a round-faced, slightly balding, bespectacled man in his midthirties. "Like any word, it's just a verbal invention—a *symbol* of our own poor devising."

"Exactly," says the first man. "And here's my point: Just as a *word* is an invention about an object or an idea, so a *story* can be an invention *about Truth*."

The other rubs his chin. "I've loved stories since I was a boy," he muses. "You know that, Tollers! Especially stories about heroism and sacrifice, death and resurrection—like the Norse myth of Balder. But when it comes to Christianity...well, that's another matter. I simply don't understand how the life and death of someone else (whoever he was) two thousand years ago can help *me* here and now."

"But don't you see, Jack?" persists his friend. "The Christian story is the greatest story of them all. Because it's the *real* story. The historical event that fulfills the tales and shows us what they mean. The *tree itself*—not just a verbal invention."

Jack stops and turns. "Are you trying to tell me that in the story of Christ...all the other stories have somehow come true?"

A week and a half later, Jack—better known to most of us as C. S. Lewis, teacher, author, defender of the Christian faith, and creator of the beloved Chronicles of Narnia—writes to his friend Arthur Greeves: "I have just passed on from believing in God to definitely believing in Christ—in Christianity. My long night talk with Tolkien had a great deal to do with it."[1]

## THE STORY ROOTED IN OUR HEARTS

Is it really reasonable to suggest that one can find images of the true God in stories, myths, and fairy tales?

Apparently that's just what Lewis did—in a sense. But *how?* What exactly did Jack and "Tollers" (J. R. R. Tolkien, author of *The Lord of the Rings*) mean when they made the appalling suggestion that "in the story of Christ…all the other stories have somehow *come true*"? Something induced these two molders and shapers of the modern Christian mind to see life-changing verbal inventions about Truth in the legends and tales they had loved as children, to discover within those stories "other names" for the Tree of Life itself. What was it?

One thing seems certain. They weren't trying to put fables and fairy stories on a par with Scripture and inspired prophecy. If you had asked, they probably would have told you that the coming of Christ *fulfilled* the hopes and dreams embodied in, say, "Snow White and the Seven Dwarfs" or "The Ugly Duckling" in a very different way than it consummated the messianic expectations of Isaiah or Micah. But fulfill them it did, said Lewis and Tolkien, and for a reason we can't afford to miss. It has to do with art and the human heart.

"God created man in His own image," declares Genesis 1:27; "in the image of God He created him." What is the heart of man but a mirror image of the One who breathed it into existence? The mirror may be cracked and marred, but it has not lost its capacity to reflect its Maker. The soul possesses no absolute life of its own. In spite of itself, it bears witness to its dependency upon Another.

And what is art but the soul's reflection, however imperfect, of the Light that gives it life and definition? This is supremely true of *story* art. In stories, the subconscious mind gives voice to some of its most deeply cherished longings. In myths and legends, men and women make desperate attempts to tell one another who they are, why they are here, where they are going, and what they are meant to do. The Tree revealed within our stories has its roots deep within the human heart.

That's why stories make particularly promising hunting grounds for spiritual treasure seekers. At least writer G. K. Chesterton thought so. And it was precisely the human connection between story art and the image of God in man that led him to this conclusion. "He who has no sympathy with myths," said Chesterton, "has no sympathy with men."[2]

> All this mythological business belongs to the poetical part of men…unless these things are appreciated artistically, they are not appreciated at all…. The life of man is a story; an adventure story; and in our vision the same is true even of the story of God.[3]

The apostle Paul had something like this in mind when, on Mars Hill, he spoke to the pagan Greeks about their "gropings" after God (Acts 17:27). "As also some of your own poets [storytellers or mythmakers] have said, 'For we are also His offspring'" (verse 28). The writer of Ecclesiastes pinpointed it, too, with his brief but telling reference to "eternity in their hearts" (Ecclesiastes

3:11). Rebel though he may be, man cannot escape the fact that he bears the stamp of God's image. Evidences of this truth, veiled or otherwise, confront him at every turn. But they come through with special clarity in the stories he tells.

## DIVINE DISCONTENT

But it's not quite enough to claim that the gospel fulfills stories simply because they are *stories*. For stories, as we know, can be either good or bad. To put it another way, some stories reflect the Divine Image only in a negative way; they bear witness to it by denying or violently defacing it. But such is not the case with fairy tales—not according to our two venerable Oxford dons. What led them to suggest the existence of a direct link between the Story that came to life in Bethlehem and tales about kings, princesses, and enchanted frogs?

To begin with, fairy tales whisper to us of our deep need. The best fairy tale is a story you *wish* would come true. And this wish, in its turn, is merely the obverse side of a confession. It's an admission that, in and of ourselves, we are incomplete.

It's significant that in Old English the word *spell* meant "story." For stories, and fairy tales in particular, cast a kind of spell over the hearer. As they work their magic, the ears of our hearts are opened, and we hear, perhaps as if for the first time, the voice of the *Imago Dei* calling us to rise up and claim our eternal birthright. In that moment, whether we're capable of articulating it or not, we suddenly realize that, as Paul wrote, "we are also His offspring" (Acts 17:28). We are roused by the stirrings of divine discontent. Like Scuffy the little tugboat, we *know* that we were "meant for bigger things."

Such rumblings of discontent have sent many a fairy-tale hero spinning off into unlikely adventures. Like the boy in the Grimm brothers' tale who was happy to get the "creeps" if only it meant experiencing something new and different. He had something in common with that "Brave Little Tailor" who went out into the world just to "try his luck." So did Jennie, the little dog who plays the central role in Maurice Sendak's modern-day fairy tale *Higglety Pigglety Pop!* Driven by these same nameless stirrings, Jennie packed her black leather bag with gold buckles, left her bowls, her pillows, and her red sweater behind, and headed out into the great unknown. Why? "I am discontented," she said, when asked for an explanation. "I want something I do not have. There must be more to life than having everything!"[4]

*There must be more to life.* That suspicion haunts each and every one of us. And not without good reason—because there really *is*.

"Man's chief end," declares the Westminster Shorter Catechism, "is to glorify God, and enjoy him forever." Thus, as Augustine says, "Our heart is restless until it repose in Thee."[5] No wonder we have this nagging feeling that something must be missing. No wonder we're unhappy with schemes and plans of our own devising. Impressive as they may be, they are but crumbling sandcastles beside the radiant fairy palaces God has prepared for us in our everlasting home.

## THE WITCH IN THE GINGERBREAD HOUSE

But fairy tales do more than tantalize and inspire with visions of beautiful and distant lands—of a country that lies "further up and further in," as in C. S. Lewis's depiction of heaven in the

Chronicles of Narnia.[6] They also remind us that the journey to that marvelous place is fraught with peril. When we travel in the company of fairy-tale heroes or heroines, we soon find that the world is far more dangerous and sinister than we had suspected. The gingerbread house may drip with sweetness, and its sugar-coated roof tiles may be studded with frosted gumdrops. But be forewarned: A witch lurks inside. And she *eats* little children.

This vision of the world as a kind of Venus's-flytrap—bright, beautiful, and malevolent—is fundamental to fairy stories. Dazzlements and delights notwithstanding, evil is an ever-present threat in the land of Faerie. In fact, the unspeakable glory and light of that land owe their power largely to the contrasting darkness and ugliness of its less attractive corners. For many grotesque and daunting dangers lie hidden in the underbrush beside the path that leads through the enchanted wood. Hags with sagging lips. Dogs with eyes as big as mill wheels. Reeking dragons. Scheming dwarfs. Cold, cruel enchantresses.

What's more, the inhabitants of the fairy world don't seem to be particularly surprised at this. They take it for granted that certain parts of the forest are to be avoided at all costs. They understand that the prince cannot rescue the sleeping princess without first hacking his way through a thick hedge of deadly thorns. They know that Dorothy *must* face the witch before returning to Kansas. In short, they lack the naiveté of those modern anchormen who still express shock and disbelief at the horrendous crimes that loom so large in the daily news. Because in Faerie, ogres cook houseguests, parents abandon children in the woods, bridegrooms dismember brides, and wicked little men steal firstborn babies almost every day. No wonder some readers find the Grimms' tales so grim and Hans Christian Andersen's stories so sad. Fairy tales, unlike a great deal of modern psychology and sociology, take sin and evil seriously. They acknowledge the reality of darkness. And they admit that it stands as an almost impassable obstacle between man and his rightful destiny. This is why we do readers—even very young readers—a disservice when we sanitize and soften the violence and brutality that figure so significantly in many traditional fairy stories. In so doing, we weaken the power of the tales and rob them of their full impact.

## GOOD NEWS

That's not the end of the story, of course. For fairy stories, as we all know—at least the best and truest examples of the genre—have happy endings. Sin may be deep and black. Evil may be as strong as a tower of adamant. The wicked Queen may know spells that will enable her to search out and destroy the heroine wherever she hides. The Dark Lord may possess powers beyond belief. But in the end they all will be defeated. Virtue and innocence will triumph at the last. That's the *good* news.

And so it happens in case after case. Cinderella rises out of oppression and obscurity to marry the prince. Gerda's love overpowers the Snow Queen's enchantments, leading to a reunion with her dear friend. Jack returns home with the giant's treasure. Snow White and Sleeping Beauty awake at the touch of a kiss.

And there's more. Not only are the good rewarded, but the wicked reap the bitter fruits of their Machiavellian machinations. What a deep sense of satisfaction we all feel when, at the climax of "Snow White and Rose Red," the conniving old dwarf falls beneath the bear's paw; when Hansel and Gretel cook the witch's goose; or when Snow White's stepmother is forced to dance in red-hot shoes until she falls down dead. In the world of Faerie, justice is always served. Evildoers get their comeuppance. Everyone lives happily ever after.

Many of us are so accustomed to this familiar feature of the fairy story that it no longer affects us as what it really is: a plot twist of the most exquisite unexpectedness. Tolkien coined a word for it: *eucatastrophe*—a "good calamity"—an overthrow or turnaround that works out for the best. This eucatastrophe, as Tolkien understood it, is a symbol of hope beyond belief. And he rightly pointed out that it is precisely *here* that the parallel between fairy tales and the gospel begins to emerge most unmistakably.

"It is not difficult to imagine the peculiar excitement and joy that one would feel," he wrote, "if any specially beautiful fairy-story were found to be 'primarily' true, its narrative to be history.… The joy would have exactly the same quality, if not the same degree, as the joy which the 'turn' in a fairy-story gives: such joy has the very taste of primary truth.… It looks forward…to the Great Eucatastrophe."[7]

## BETTER NEWS

But the good news doesn't stop there. It gets even better.

Fairy stories do not merely tell us that good triumphs over evil. That would be a fairly generic message, and fairy tales don't deal in generics. No, their tonic is far more bracing, far more astringent, far more specific than that. Fairy tales spell out the details. They describe for us exactly *how* the light prevails and dispels the darkness. And it's at this point that their character as foreshadowings of the gospel—the *god spell* or Good Story we've waited so long to hear—becomes most pronounced.

First, fairy tales declare that the victory over evil is accomplished by means of a radical *turning of the tables*. They make the bold and shocking claim that this battle is fought not by might, nor by power, but in weakness; not by kings and warriors, but by the humble and meek; not with sword and shield, but with luck and pluck. In other words, they proclaim a message of breathtakingly amazing grace.

Examples are almost too many to enumerate. Jack's mother thinks him a simpleton and a fool for taking a handful of beans in exchange for the cow…until those beans enable him to bring home a hen that lays golden eggs. Cinderella is despised, rejected, and consigned to the ash heap like the lowliest of servants…but her foot alone fits the glass slipper. Kings, dukes, earls, and knights cannot draw the sword from the stone…but Wart, Sir Ector's scrawny foster son, does so with ease. It's always the youngest and smallest of the farmer's seven sons who defeats the ogre, climbs the glass mountain, or wins the princess—just as David, unlikeliest of the sons of Jesse, was anointed to be Israel's greatest king. The first become last and the last, first.

But this victory is not won without great cost. Grace may be amazing, but it is not cheap. And this, too, is something that fairy tales illustrate through powerful, unforgettable imagery.

"My life," wrote Hans Christian Andersen in the opening lines of his *Autobiography*, "is a beautiful fairy tale."[8] If so, it was a fairy tale filled with dark ironies, painful losses, unexpected twists, and unavoidable sacrifices. Andersen's early life was marked by hardship, poverty, bereavement, and disappointment. As a student and a struggling young writer, he knew what it was like to live in a freezing garret and subsist on gruel. Even as a mature and successful author, he was shy and awkward and found it difficult to relate to other adults in social settings. His love for Jenny Lind, a popular singer of the day, went unexpressed and unrequited. In reflecting on this rather tragic aspect of Andersen's personal story—and the indelible mark it has left upon his literary work—critic Naomi Lewis says, "Our wishes, it seems...are fulfilled more often than we expect, but not always in the way we desire. There is always a price to be paid."[9]

*A price to be paid.* Perhaps this is why redemptive suffering plays such an important role in Andersen's world. Such suffering is in the very atmosphere his imaginary heroes and heroines breathe. It's the backdrop against which they play out their memorable histories.

For example, in "The Wild Swans," young Elise endures toil, pain, misunderstanding, persecution, imprisonment, and near death in her attempts to rescue her twelve brothers from an evil spell. Rather than harm a hair of her beloved prince's head, the Little Mermaid casts away her last dying hope and becomes foam on the surface of the sea. The Steadfast Tin Soldier bears all things, believes all things, hopes all things, endures all things for love.

Who can ponder all this without being reminded of the great Suffering Redeemer? The One who paid the price for us all? "A man of sorrows," Isaiah calls Him, "and acquainted with grief" (Isaiah 53:3). A man who, like Andersen's Ugly Duckling, "was despised, and we did not esteem Him" (verse 3).

Surely He has borne our griefs
And carried our sorrows;
Yet we esteemed Him stricken,
Smitten by God, and afflicted.
But He was wounded for our transgressions,
He was bruised for our iniquities;
The chastisement for our peace was upon Him,
And by His stripes we are healed. (Isaiah 53:4-5)

## THE HAPPIEST ENDING

Strange, isn't it, that *this* should be the sort of thing that finally won an intellect like C. S. Lewis to the Christian faith? Yet so it was. As a result of that "long night talk with Tolkien," he came to realize that the thing he had been groping after all his life—the thing he had perceived so clearly in myths, poems, fables, sagas, and fairy stories—was actually *there* to be encountered in all of its glorious reality. As he expressed it in one of his later writings:

> The heart of Christianity is a myth which is also a fact.... It happens—at a particular date, in a particular place, followed by definable historical consequences.... By becoming fact it does not cease to be myth: that is the miracle.[10]

Tolkien said much the same thing:

> I would venture to say that approaching the Christian
> Story from this direction, it has long been my feeling
> (a joyous feeling) that God redeemed the corrupt making-
> creatures, men, in a way fitting to this aspect, as to others,

of their strange nature. The Gospels contain a fairy-story, or a story of a larger kind which embraces all the essence of fairy-stories.... But this story has entered History and the primary world; the desire and aspiration of sub-creation has been raised to the fulfillment of Creation.[11]

In the gospel of Christ, Tolkien and Lewis discovered the Tree of Life—not the verbal symbol, but the reality itself—standing unveiled before their marveling eyes. The wish had been granted, the quest fulfilled. Best of all, the price—the unthinkably high and costly price—had been paid...paid in full by the greatest hero and adventurer of them all, the Lamb slain from the foundation of the world. It was the happiest of all happy endings.

## READING THROUGH CHRIST-COLORED GLASSES

"Mythology," wrote G. K. Chesterton, "is a *search*."[12] In the pages that follow we will join the ranks of those who have pursued this imaginative quest down through the ages. In the style of Tolkien and Lewis, we will travel the road that leads through the land of make-believe, keeping an eye out for spiritual truths along the way. We will examine a selection of folk tales, fairy stories, and literary fantasies through "Christ-colored glasses"—everything from the ancient and obscure to the familiar and relatively modern—just to see what we might see. Every chapter will begin with a brief retelling of a tale or a strategic scene from that tale. Each retelling will be followed by a short reflection or meditation inspired by the story's imagery and plot line.

As we journey together, please bear this thought in mind: Our purpose is not to analyze or interpret. At no point will we attempt to take fairy tales captive to a particular point of view, nor will we presume to tell anyone what they "really mean." Our goal is at once much simpler and far more formidable than that: to share a vision that emerges—or *can* emerge—when the fancies of the human heart are viewed through the eyes of Christ-centered faith.

# BREAKTHROUGH

*Close Encounters with the World Beyond*

"Thomas the Rhymer" from Scottish folklore

*True Thomas lay on Huntlie bank;*
*A ferlie he spied wi' his ee...*

It happened on a day at the beginning of summer, that time when the sun rises early and lingers late and sweet, dewy nights string the cobwebs with pearls of glowing moonsheen; when the hawthorn blooms alongside the jeweled blue harebell and the flame-red poppy; when the veil between the Seen and the Unseen, thin and sheer at any time, is sometimes drawn aside or even rent—usually without the slightest warning.

It was the season of the Fairy Raid—the time when the folk of the Sidhe walk abroad in the world of men.

At such a time, all unheeding, Thomas the Rhymer, poet of Ercildoune, reclined at ease on Huntlie bank, dreaming dreams and composing pleasant nothings in the twilight. He nibbled at the end of his quill and lay back in the grass, musing. Then he sat up, spread out his parchment, and began to write:

Her shirt was o' the grass-green silk,
    Her mantle o' the velvet fyne;

> At ilka tett of her horse's mane,
>> Hung fifty siller bells and nine.[13]

Thomas smiled, pleased with his own versifying. Shifting his pen from hand to hand, he smoothed the parchment and peered into the gathering dusk. All at once his smile faded. He rubbed his eyes and stared.

*Could it be?* He blinked and stared again. His parchment and quill dropped to the grass. He struggled to his feet.

Such unearthly beauty! From whence had she come? He'd seen no sign of her approach. He'd heard nothing…nothing at all, until the delicate chiming of the tiny silver bells woke him, as if out of an agelong trance.

"Greetings, Thomas," she said in a soothing, musical voice.

He nodded mutely. The bells, he now saw, hung tinkling from the braided mane of her nimble white horse. She was indescribably fair, in a gown of green velvet, with a garland of summer flowers in her abundant golden hair. Her face shone as if with a brilliance of its own, a light so keen that he was forced to avert his eyes.

Thomas snapped shut his gaping mouth. *Impossible!* he thought. And yet there she was—the very woman he'd been describing, not half a minute before, in his metrical toying and trifling! Unthinkably, his rhymes had come to life!

He knelt before her, pulled off his cap, and bowed his head. "Are you…" He faltered. "Are you the Queen of Heaven?"

> "O no, O no, Thomas," she said,
>> "That name does not belang to me;

I am but the Queen of fair Elfland,
>   That am hither come to visit thee."[14]

His heart turned to water. His name, his place, his upbring-
ing, and his kin—these things he remembered no more. He
could feel her blue-green eyes burning a hole in the top of his
head as the tips of her cool satin fingers touched his hand. He
looked up into her face. It was clear, shining, and painfully beautiful in the shade of the Eildon-tree. Without thinking, he got to
his feet, took a strand of her yellow hair between his fingers, and
kissed her red lips.

She laughed—a laugh like the bubbling of a gentle brook—
and softly thrust him away. "And now," said she with a smile,
"you must come with me, Thomas. You must come with me to
the Land of Faerie:"

And ye maun serve me seven years,
>   Thro' weal or woe as may chance to be.[15]

He stood speechless, gazing at her beauty. Snared, captivated,
overruled completely. She reached down and pulled him up into
the saddle behind her. Flinging her head back, she whistled to her
milk-white steed. Away they flew, swifter than the wind, while
the chiming of the bells faded into the folds of the creeping mists
beyond Huntlie bank.

It was seven years before anyone saw Thomas in the neighborhood of Berwickshire again.

When he returned, it was as a changed man.

When he returned, it was not as *Thomas the Rhymer,* but as *True Thomas:* poet, prophet, and seer.

⚜

A *ferlie.* That, according to the ancient poet, is what Thomas saw beneath the Eildon-tree.

Just what is a ferlie? Good question. Because the phenomenon itself has been forgotten almost as completely as the old Scots word used to describe it.

A ferlie (or *fairlie*—from the Old English *faer,* meaning "danger," and *faerlic,* "unexpected") is a sudden apparition, a sight or experience so strange, so unnerving, and so disarming that words fail to do it justice. It's a portent, a marvel, a wake-up call. A breakthrough from beyond the veil that normally screens the unseen world from human eyes.

That unseen world—the world not only of powers, principalities, angels, and archangels, but of the immortal souls of women and men—exists as surely and as certainly as the invisible air we breathe. According to the story of Thomas, it is a world of terrible beauty. It's also dangerously and unpredictably dynamic —a realm of vibrant, pulsating life that constantly threatens to overflow its boundaries and burst in upon the unwary without the slightest warning. And it is close to us, closer than we can imagine. At any given moment it is no more than a short, unforeseeable step away.

This, according to fairy lore, is the great and fearsome possibility that hangs over the head of each and every mortal during every hour of his or her fleeting existence: the possibility of an instant encounter with the invisible Life that beats at the very heart of the universe. For those who have eyes to see and ears to hear, that experience lurks around every corner. In the words of poet Francis Thompson:

> The angels keep their ancient places;—
> Turn but a stone, and start a wing!
> 'Tis ye, 'tis your estrangèd faces,
> That miss the many-splendoured thing.[16]

It's a basic biblical concept, this idea of the ferlie, this notion of a transporting and transforming meeting with the life-shattering reality of the world beyond. "Am I a God near at hand," asks the Lord, "and not a God afar off?" (Jeremiah 23:23). We know the answer. God, as the apostle Paul told the Athenians, "is not far from each one of us" (Acts 17:27). In fact, He is even nearer than near. The invisible God, like the Fairy Queen in the story "Thomas the Rhymer," has taken the initiative to withdraw the parting veil, to step out of eternity and into the world of time and space. He has burst in upon our drowsy musings like a lightning bolt out of the blue. This is the essence of the Christian gospel.

The prophet Ezekiel knew this. He, too, spied a ferlie while minding his own business beside the riverbank one day.

> Then I looked, and behold, a whirlwind was coming out of the north, a great cloud with raging fire engulfing itself; and brightness was all around it and radiating out of its midst like the color of amber, out of the midst of the fire....

Like the appearance of a rainbow in a cloud on a
rainy day, so was the appearance of the brightness all
around it. This was the appearance of the likeness of the
glory of the LORD.

So when I saw it, I fell on my face. (Ezekiel 1:4,28)

The apostle John saw something similar while serving time
on the isle of Patmos:

I saw seven golden lampstands, and in the midst of the
seven lampstands One like the Son of Man, clothed with
a garment down to the feet and girded about the chest
with a golden band. His head and hair were white like
wool, as white as snow, and His eyes like a flame of fire;
His feet were like fine brass, as if refined in a furnace, and
His voice as the sound of many waters; He had in His
right hand seven stars, out of His mouth went a sharp
two-edged sword, and His countenance was like the sun
shining in its strength. And when I saw Him, I fell at His
feet as dead. (Revelation 1:12-17)

*I fell at His feet as dead.* If we're to believe the testimony of
firsthand witnesses, a ferlie invariably affects the beholder in precisely this way. What else should we expect when human darkness
comes face to face with the beauty of eternal light? This is a close
encounter so wonderful and fearful, so perilous and lovely, that
anyone who experiences it must either change or die.

If only we could see it! If only, like the prophet Elisha's servant, the eyes of our hearts might be opened to perceive the real-

ity of our position—to behold the mountains round about us "full of horses and chariots of fire" (2 Kings 6:17). If only, in Thompson's phrase (from stanza one of the poem quoted above), we could see the invisible, touch the intangible, and know the unknowable. Then indeed, we, like Thomas, would find ourselves unalterably changed.

To spy a ferlie like the ones Thomas the Rhymer, Ezekiel the prophet, or John the Revelator perceived is to experience pure, unmerited grace. For the partition between the Seen and the Unseen realms, be it ever so thin and liable to shakings and stirrings, can only be breached from the other side. When this happens, Christians speak of the miracle of divine revelation.

No one has seen God at any time. The only begotten Son,
who is in the bosom of the Father, He has declared Him.
(John 1:18)

The incarnation of Christ—this is the greatest ferlie of them all. For in this once-for-all, never-to-be-repeated historical event, God has torn the separating veil from top to bottom and removed it altogether (Matthew 27:51).

# ENCHANTED FOREST

*The Mystery of God's Creation*

*Phantastes* by George MacDonald

*Every tree,*
*O'ershadowing with gloom,*
*Seems to cover thee,*
*Secret, dark, love-still'd,*
*In a holy room*
*Silence-filled.*

—PHANTASTES, CHAPTER 6

A faint, musical note of trickling water. A passing breath of cool dawn air. A stillness, sudden and arresting as quiet thunder after the night's restless dreams. A silence, gentle but alive with the barely perceptible motion of dappled light among leaves.

Anodos stirred. Dimly he became aware of an odd sensation, as if the outdoors had somehow come inside. Was it raining? Had he left the window open before going to bed? He couldn't rightly remember. With a groan, he pulled the coverlet up over his head and pressed his face into the pillow. *Too early,* he thought.

There it was again!—that insistent *splash, plash, tinkle*—like the babble of a rising mountain spring. Was he dreaming still? The sound seemed to be coming from the basin in the corner— the green marble washbasin on the green marble stand, where every morning he rinsed off the residue of the night. Throwing off the blankets, Anodos sat up and looked across the room.

Marvel of marvels! Water was indeed bubbling up over the lip of the green bowl and pouring down in a crystal fountain. It was splashing and spattering off the base of the pedestal, flowing in a tiny rivulet down over the carpet—the carpet he himself had designed on a pattern of daisies and violets and tender young grass.

Anodos blinked and looked closer. Was it his imagination? Or was that actually grass waving to and fro? Yes—there could be no mistaking it now. The tiny blades really were undulating, dancing for joy in the small, clear ripples at the edge of the growing stream. They were fresh and green and very real. The water gurgled past his bed, and he noticed that the ornately carved legs of the black oak dressing table were alive with the climbing tendrils of clematis and ivy.

More stirrings. His glance was drawn upward to the bed's canopy and curtains, which were woven in the likeness of leaves and twining branches. Another puff of the morning breeze, and the branches and leaves began rustling and swaying above his head.

Anodos jumped out of bed. The cool wetness of dewy grass against his bare feet came as a sudden shock. His thoughts were racing. What could it all mean? Then he remembered the vision he'd seen the previous evening. Out of the hidden compartment at the back of the old desk, a tiny, lovely lady had appeared and spoken to him in strange, bewildering words. It all came back to him clearly now. Had it truly been only a dream, as he'd supposed?

By the time he finished dressing, he was standing beneath the lowest boughs of a great oak tree, looking up through layer upon canopied layer of fluttering, glancing leaves that rose heavenward in gilt-edged ranks, high into the blue air and the swelling morning light. To the east, the rays of the rising sun shone like molten gold between the receding pillars of the trunks. Before his feet lay a muddy, mossy track that led away through the dark stems and into the shadowy depths of a dense green forest.

Fear, apprehension, and the thrill of a nameless challenge filled his heart. Squaring his shoulders, he set foot upon the path and followed it into the wood, recalling all the while the tiny lady's parting benediction:

"Tomorrow you shall find the way into Fairy Land."

❧

If you've traveled much in Faerie, you're probably acquainted with the Enchanted Forest. It's a familiar feature of most fantasy landscapes. And not without good reason, for even in the real world, woods and forests have a way of weaving a spell over those who venture beneath their shadowed caves.

It's difficult to explain this feeling of awe that steals over us when we enter a forested glade. It has about it something of the mystery of a well-told tale, something of the reverential hush of a columned cathedral. Perhaps it's just the solitude, silence, and secrecy that dwell deep in the heart of a tangled dell. Perhaps it's a by-product of the green shadows and flitting sunspots that play so elusively over the feathered ferns. Whatever it is, it certainly flows in some measure from that sense of nameless anticipation that awaits every visitor to the wildwood. After all, one never knows what might be lurking behind that next tree.

For Anodos (whose name comes from a Greek word meaning "upward" or "inland journey"), protagonist of George MacDonald's "Faerie Romance" *Phantastes,* the forest turns out to be the road to Fairy Land itself: a passageway leading up and out of the dull humdrum of daily doubt and disbelief and straight into the trackless marvels and miracles of a fairer, richer world.

Anodos, like the boy Max in Maurice Sendak's *Where the Wild Things Are,* awakes one morning to find that his bedroom has been transformed into a wooded wonderland. Like Lucy, Susan, Peter, and Edmund in C. S. Lewis's *The Lion, the Witch, and the Wardrobe,* he plunges into that forest and follows the light that gleams between its dusky boles and branches. In every case the woodland turns out to be something more than a mere collection of trees. It's the road to adventure, the gateway to unimaginable marvels.

Can anything of value be gleaned from this notion of the forest as a kind of antechamber to the supernatural realm? As an in-between place where mere human beings often find themselves delightfully and frightfully out of their element? What was it that inspired C. S. Lewis to seize upon this image of the "Wood Between the Worlds" in constructing the legendary history of Narnia?[17]

The answer to that question turns out to be surprisingly biblical. For in its own childishly faltering and incomplete way, this myth of the Enchanted Woodland reflects something more than a mere psychological fact. It is also strongly reminiscent of a recurring scriptural theme—what we might call the contrast between the *garden* and the *forest.*

God planted a garden eastward in Eden and appointed a man

and a woman to tend and till it (Genesis 2:8-25). Familiar and comfortable, peaceful and practical, cultivated and eminently useful—the garden was all this and more. Within the garden, man and woman found everything suitable and needful for human life.

But beyond Eden, in the wilds and wastes outside, there God made the forest. He populated it with outlandish, extravagant, and untamable beasts, creatures who neither knew nor cared for man: hyraxes and camelopards, onagers and oliphaunts, emus and ostriches, basilisks and wild boars. He filled it with wonders and marvels that had nothing to do with the advancement of agriculture, the promotion of industry, or the development of commerce. At the farthest end of the forest He raised the mountains, and beyond the mountains He spread the seas. There in the depths of ocean He caused great leviathan to dwell. Then God looked upon all these fearful things He had made. And God said it was *good.*

God intended humankind for the garden. Though expelled from the garden as a result of sin, we nevertheless remember it and long to return to it. The forest, on the other hand, is that place where man has never really belonged. It's that segment of God's world where he remains a small, insignificant stranger: a visitor, a tourist, a babe in the woods. The forest, in this sense, includes all the howling deserts, all the wind-blasted rocky fastnesses, all the restless leagues of the sea, and all the endless reaches of outer space that refuse to yield humanity so much as a square inch of ground upon which to stand. It's that vast human-free zone, that wild, uncharted reserve within the grand scheme of creation where there can be no question of human self-sufficiency, let alone human dominion.

It's in this sense that the forest becomes a realm of enchant-ment…a passageway to the Otherworld…perhaps even a stair-way to heaven itself. For the forest is a place where we are forced to acknowledge that God is God and we are not, where the Lord alone, shrouded in unapproachable light, rejoices in the inex-haustible goodness and exuberant variety of His wild and parti-colored world.

This idea of the forest as God's special laughing place—a place outside the camp and beyond the city walls of human habi-tation—casts a certain light on some otherwise puzzling aspects of the biblical account.

It explains, for instance, why Moses and the children of Israel had to leave the great cities of Egypt and strike out into the desert in order to meet the Lord. And why Elijah had to hike up the skirts of his robe and run all the way down to Mount Horeb (Hebrew for "desolation" or "wilderness") before he could see the wind and the fire and hear the still, small voice. It explains why Jesus Himself could not begin His work on earth until He had spent forty days and nights fasting in the wilderness. For Anodos, the forest became the path to Fairy Land. For believers, it is the road to the Land of Promise.

This is why God takes Job into the forest when it's time to settle accounts and set the record straight:

> Where were you when I laid the foundations of the
> earth?…
> Tell Me, if you know all this.…
> Who has divided a channel for the overflowing water,
> Or a path for the thunderbolt,

To cause it to rain on a land where there is no one,
A wilderness in which there is no man?...
Can you hunt the prey for the lion,
Or satisfy the appetite of the young lions,
When they crouch in their dens,
Or lurk in their lairs to lie in wait?
    (Job 38:4,18,25-26,39-40)

The psalmist expresses much the same idea in slightly different language:

Every beast of the forest is Mine,
And the cattle on a thousand hills.
I know all the birds of the mountains,
And the wild beasts of the field are Mine.
If I were hungry, I would not tell you;
For the world is Mine, and all its fullness.
    (Psalm 50:10-12)

No wonder storytellers have always been so taken with the mystery of the forest. No wonder our ancestors found it almost impossible to resist the idea that wastes and woodlands verge on the very doorstep of the universe itself. They realized that God's creation is far too big and far too beautiful to comprehend or control. And they enshrined that bit of wisdom for us, perhaps more effectively than anywhere else, in the fantasies and fairy tales they invented.

# Magic Word

## The Power of Speech

"Ali Baba and the Forty Thieves" from *Arabian Nights*

*Going up to the door, he said, "Open, Sesame!"*
*as the captain had done. Instantly the door flew open.*

Ali Baba tossed one last stick of wood on the donkey's back, then strapped the bundle down with a braided leather cord. Wiping the sweat from his eyes with the tail of his turban, he shouldered his ax and gave the beast a loud slap on the flank.

"Home, you long-eared, fly-bitten, hairy-muzzled son of a baggage trolley!" he shouted. He smacked the donkey again to emphasize the point.

Ali Baba had a tendency to be cruel to his animals. He knew it. But he consoled himself with the thought that he was not entirely to blame. *A man must have some means of working out his frustrations,* he thought. In the best of all possible worlds, he'd have been smacking Cassim instead.

Their worthless father had died, leaving Ali Baba and his brother, Cassim, with nothing. Absolutely nothing! Not long afterward, Cassim, that prince of dogs, had had the good fortune to marry a woman of wealth. If Cassim had been as rich in kindness and good sense as he was in dumb luck, he might have shared some of that gold and silver with his poor, hard-working brother. Then again, maybe that was expecting too much.

Ali Baba pulled out a filthy linen handkerchief and wiped his brow again. Even here in the wooded foothills the air was hot. *When I get home,* he thought, *the first thing I'll do is find a cool spot in the shade. Then I'll—*

He stopped. He listened. What was that sound? He peered between the trunks of the trees. Smoke? Could the forest be burning? But no—the more he squinted at it, the more he felt that the low-lying cloud in the distance had the appearance of dust as it rises and spreads in the wake of galloping riders. He dashed ahead to a small open space beside a huge outcrop of rock.

Robbers! He could see them plainly now: horsemen—twenty, thirty, maybe forty of them—riding hard, making straight for the spot where he was standing! Without hesitation, he drove the donkey into the brush and shimmied up a tree. There among the branches, shivering with fear, he awaited the approach of the horsemen.

Within a matter of moments the whole troop came thundering into the clearing. With loud laughs and rude shouts, they reined up just in front of the large rock. Then their captain, a dark-bearded, scar-faced man of terrifying height, swung off his mount, threw his black cloak over his shoulder, and strode up to the stone.

"Open, Sesame!" he trumpeted.

Ali Baba stared open-mouthed as, magically, a door opened in the rock. At a signal from their captain, the other riders dismounted and filed through the opening. Then the door shut behind them, and every trace of its existence vanished.

Ali Baba waited and watched. Not until dusk did the robbers emerge from the cave. When at last each and every rider had remounted and thundered away, he climbed down from his hiding place, stiff and aching in every joint. Then, cautiously as a hunted rabbit, he edged forward until he stood facing the great gray rock.

"Open…," he said in a small, quivering, half-apologetic voice. Then louder: "Open! Open, Sesame!"

A loud, sharp *crack!* resounded from somewhere deep within the rock. Seams opened in the face of the gray stone, outlining the shape of a wide rectangular door. With a scraping, grating sound, the door swung slowly open.

Ali Baba stepped into the delicious coolness of the cavern. As his eyes adjusted to the light, a vision of such wonder emerged that he had to pinch himself to make sure he wasn't dreaming.

The cave was filled with untold wealth! Rich bales of silk, bundles of costly brocade, and rolls of brightly woven Persian carpets were stacked high on every side. Piles of gold coins, jewels, and silver vessels of every imaginable size and shape covered the floor, standing in heaps as tall as a man. Polished swords and shields like bright mirrors hung from the dark stone walls.

Ali Baba caught his breath and blinked. Here was treasure beyond his wildest dreams!

*If only Cassim could see me now!* he thought.

"Sticks and stones can break my bones, but words can never hurt me." That's what they used to say on the school playground.

But in the world of fable and fairy tale, words can do just about anything. Words break down impassable barriers and open doors in walls of solid granite. They change pumpkins into coaches, turn mice into horses, transform scullery maids into princesses. At a word, a king's son becomes a frog and a frog a king's son. Farmers, tinkers, and tailors fly through the air, walk on the bottom of the sea, pull down fortresses, and send three-headed giants sprawling—all by the power of words.

Words, in the land of Faerie, determine destiny and recast the shape of the world. Words alter the course of people's lives.

Consider Ali Baba: His life took a radical turn when he happened to overhear two little words—"Open, Sesame!"—while shambling home from work through the woods one day. With his own eyes he witnessed what those two little words could do. And when he dared to repeat them himself, however falteringly, they had the effect of skyrocketing him to an entirely new and different plane of existence. He spoke, and a door opened in the rock. After that, nothing could be the same.

*Abracadabra!... Alakazam!... Bibbidi-bobbidi-boo!* Anyone who knows and loves fantasy is familiar with the motif of the magic word. Author J. K. Rowling uses the device freely in her Harry Potter novels—though it's "Alohomora!" rather than "Open, Sesame!" that gets young Hermione Granger past locked doors and into secret chambers. As any Potter fan knows, the halls of Hogwarts are simply alive with the sounds of magic words.

Where does it come from, this fascination with the power of particular words? And why does it figure so prominently in the folklore of so many different lands? It would be easy to explain it as a holdover from the dark practices of the medieval alchemists and conjurers, to condemn it out of hand as a distasteful relic of the ancient black arts. But this is overly simplistic. Even the spells of the enchanters preserve a memory of something far too important to miss: the mystery of language itself.

Have you ever stopped to think about it? Human speech is a downright miracle. As a matter of fact, anthropologists tell us that language is the one thing that most decisively distinguishes human beings from the animals. And upon reflection, it's not hard to see why. To speak is to express the soul. To converse with a neighbor, to derive meaning from a series of symbols on a page, to establish a meaningful link from mind to mind—these are truly godlike activities.

Speech is far more than mere "sound and fury." On the contrary, this endlessly varied flow of stops, sibilants, and voicings always signifies *something*. It has the power to build up or to tear down. It can heal or kill. At some moments it assumes the form of a tender protestation of love, at others that of a blistering barrage of hate. It calls for war; it urges peace. How did such a fearful and wonderful thing as language ever come into the world? Surely there is a sense in which every word is a magic word.

That's why Jesus warned His disciples to weigh their words carefully. Words matter. They have the power to impact our lives and the lives of others in ways we hardly dare to imagine: "If you have faith as a mustard seed, you will say to this mountain, 'Move from here to there,' and it will move; and nothing will be impossible for you" (Matthew 17:20). So formidable, in fact, is the power and virtue attached to our words that it would not be an exaggeration to claim that they can either make us or break us. In the final analysis, says Jesus, everything boils down to words:

But I say to you that for every idle word men may speak,
they will give account of it in the day of judgment. For by
your words you will be justified, and by your words you
will be condemned. (Matthew 12:36-37)

Therefore whatever you have spoken in the dark will be
heard in the light, and what you have spoken in the ear
in inner rooms will be proclaimed on the housetops.
(Luke 12:3)

James expresses this same idea in even more striking terms:
"If anyone does not stumble in word, he is a perfect man, able
also to bridle the whole body" (James 3:2). And Paul, in one of
the Bible's best known and most classically stated presentations of
the gospel message, asserts that words are absolutely essential to
saving faith:

But what does it say? "The word is near you, in your
mouth and in your heart" (that is, the word of faith which
we preach): that if you confess with your mouth the Lord
Jesus and believe in your heart that God has raised Him
from the dead, you will be saved. For with the heart one
believes unto righteousness, and with the mouth confession is made unto salvation. (Romans 10:8-10)

From a biblical perspective, then, words are every bit as powerful—every bit as magical, if you will—as Ali Baba found them to
be. And this should not surprise us. After all, Genesis teaches that
human beings, the race of speakers, have been created in the

image of the greatest Magician and Conjurer of all, the One who called forth all things out of nothing merely by the fiat of His Word. That Word is not only powerful, but all-powerful. That Word, in the phrase of Martin Luther's great hymn, is above all earthly powers. It creates and destroys, judges and justifies. It goes forth out of His mouth like a two-edged sword (Revelation 1:16), "piercing even to the division of soul and spirit, and of joints and marrow" (Hebrews 4:12).

What is the secret of the wonder-working power of God's Word? Simply this: His Word is the embodiment of Himself. Nothing more, nothing less. The great fact of history is that, in and through His Word, He has personally come to make His dwelling with His people.

> In the beginning was the Word, and the Word was with God, and the Word was God....
>
> And the Word became flesh and dwelt among us, and we beheld His glory, the glory as of the only begotten of the Father, full of grace and truth. (John 1:1,14)

The tale of Ali Baba's life-changing experience with the power of words is reflected and brought to fulfillment in the life of the Christian. For the Word Made Flesh, appearing in the fullness of time, opens the door of heavenly riches to all who speak His name, believing in its power.

# FORBIDDEN ROOM

*Heeding the Word of Warning*

"Bluebeard" from Charles Perrault and the Brothers Grimm

> *Here are the keys to the entire castle. You can open*
> *all the rooms and look at everything.*
> *But I forbid you to open one particular room,*
> *which this little golden key can unlock.*
> *If you open it, you will pay for it with your life.*

The clatter of the lock was like the rattle in a dying man's throat. So irksome, so annoying—*so maddening!* Why couldn't she get the little key to turn? The harder she tried, the more violently her hand trembled.

*Why so nervous? Why so afraid?* She knew very well why. Beads of cold sweat trickled from her ivory-smooth forehead and down a stray lock of dark hair that lay rakishly along her left cheek. She felt faint. Reaching up, she brushed aside the strand of hair and sighed heavily. Then, drawing the key from the lock, she leaned her shoulder against the richly carved oak door. For a moment she paused to rest…and reconsider.

Why was she doing this? What in the world could have possessed her to take such a chance? His instructions couldn't have been clearer: "The house is yours to do with as you wish. *But stay out of this one room!*" That was plain enough, wasn't it? What had driven her to defy him so brazenly?

It wasn't that she disliked him or that he had ever given her cause for discontent. He was as kind and soft-spoken as he was generous and open handed. And he was fabulously rich. Never once had the young wife wanted for a single thing since the day of her arrival in her husband's many-towered manor house. Their life together had been unruffled and serene.

Still, there was something about him…something that made her uneasy in quiet, private moments. It was hard to put a finger on it…

Maybe it was his beard.

Stepping away from the door, she stared down at the little golden key in the palm of her hand. *How is it possible to love, cherish, and obey a man so different from other men?* she wondered. The color of his beard—that eerie blue—was simply bizarre. How, then, could his instructions and commands be regarded with anything but suspicion?

Then again, it might have had nothing to do with the beard at all. Maybe it was just her curiosity. What could he be hiding behind that door? What was he trying to keep from her? Riches, silver and gold, no doubt. Indescribable treasures and wonders that he was hoarding for his own enjoyment. Surely a man with a blue beard must be inordinately selfish.

In any case, she'd grown weary, unspeakably weary, of waiting for him to come home from his long journey. With a sharp twinge of resentment she recalled the awful blueness of his beard, stark against the redness of his face, as he finished packing his bags and turned to her with a severe expression, shaking his finger at her like a father scolding a little child. *Go anywhere you like. But keep out of this room. If you don't, you will die.*

What was he thinking? What did he expect her to do, alone with the servants in this grand old house, with nothing for her amusement but fine clothes and glittering trinkets, nothing but food and wine and games and endless diversions? How unreasonable for a supposedly loving husband to withhold a secret from his wife. The more she thought about it, the more she felt that she simply had to have a look inside.

She bit her lip. Then she thrust the key into the hole. Her jaw was set, her hand steady, her determination sure. The key turned. The tumblers in the lock clicked over. Slowly, slowly the door creaked open...

But *oh!* the horror—the absolute *horror* of it!

Recoiling from the darkness, the filth, and the stench, from the red terror of it all, she stumbled backward as the door swung in. Then, recovering, she lunged for the key and yanked it from the lock with dead, numb fingers. She fumbled. The glittering golden object fell from her hand and splashed in the blood on the floor.

*Why, oh why had she dared to disobey?*

Stifling a scream, she picked up the key and fled.

❧

Wondering what the young bride saw when she opened that door and looked inside that chamber? If so, perhaps it's because you're a lot like her.

We're *all* a lot like her. That's the point of her story. It's *our* story. That's why the tale of "Bluebeard," for all its less attractive aspects, is worth a closer look.

If you want to know exactly what she found in the room, you'll have to dig up a copy of Charles Perrault's *Contes du temps passé* or a faithful translation of the *Kinder- und Hausmärchen* of the brothers Grimm and read the tale of "Bluebeard" for yourself. But be prepared. It's not a pretty picture. As a reward for her curiosity, this unfortunate young lady found herself confronted with a roomful of bloody corpses and the horrifying prospect of a cruel and violent death.

But there's an important sense in which the blood and gore and bizarreness of Bluebeard's crimes are beside the point. For our purposes, the important thing is to gain a handle on the young wife's problem and recognize its application to our own experience. For one thing, we know that she deliberately chose to disregard solemn, specific instructions. For another, it's clear that the result of her choice was something altogether dreadful.

That last point deserves to be underscored. Make no mistake about it: "Bluebeard" is not a tale for the fainthearted. What that young wife saw in the forbidden room was terrible indeed. So terrible and devastating that, afterward, she'd have given anything never to have discovered it at all. What she saw shattered her world and very nearly led to her death. And the imprint it left upon her brain must have haunted her for the rest of her life.

Why is it that the forbidden room is always the room we simply *must* see? The forbidden gold the treasure we *have* to touch? The forbidden fruit the food we just can't live without? That, at any rate, is the way it usually turns out in fairy stories.

Fairy tales are filled with prohibitions of one kind or another, dire warnings to stay away from this or that place, avoid this or that person, refrain from this or that mode of speech or behavior. They're also heavily populated with otherwise sensible individuals who somehow find it impossible to follow simple instructions, people who just can't seem to resist the temptation to unlock that door, peek inside that cupboard, or eat that little piece of cake. All this in spite of the fact that the consequences attached to the prohibitions are usually as severe as can be imagined. In nearly every case, the stakes are mortally high. It's a matter of life and death.

If all of this sounds familiar to students of the Bible, it's for a good reason. In essence, what we have here is the story of Eden, the tragic tale of humanity's temptation and fall. Here again is the test to which mankind was put at the beginning of time, the test each of us faces every single day: "Everything you see here is yours to enjoy. Everything, without limit. Everything, that is, *except this one tree.* If you touch this tree, something bad will happen."

> Then the LORD God took the man and put him in the
> garden of Eden to tend and keep it. And the LORD God
> commanded the man, saying, "Of every tree of the garden
> you may freely eat; but of the tree of the knowledge of
> good and evil you shall not eat, for in the day that you eat
> of it, you shall surely die." (Genesis 2:15-17)

People often ask, "Why are there so many negatives in the Bible? Why so many 'Thou shalt nots'?" The truly surprising thing, of course, is that there are so few—and that, in spite of their fewness, we still find it so hard to take them seriously.

At Sinai, God gave the Hebrews ten fundamental rules. No

more than can be counted on the fingers of a child's two hands. Of those ten, only eight are negative ("Remember the Sabbath Day" and "Honor your father and mother" are positively stated). Eight simple little "Thou shalt nots." And yet before Moses had time to get down from the mountain, each and every one of those commandments had been broken by the people in the camp below. What's wrong with this picture?

Let's face it. The amazing thing about God's governance is the shocking degree of freedom He grants to His children. The incredible lack of restrictive regulations. Yes, a few prohibitions have been put in place to mark out the perimeter of our play area. A list of rules has been posted on the wall to give some much-needed definition to our otherwise unimpeded liberty. But what we fail to notice in the midst of all this is just how extensive our Father's big backyard really is. We miss the joy of tumbling in the grass and splashing through the stream because, like defiant toddlers, we're always huddled up against the fence, testing the boundaries. Like stupid sheep and cattle, we're forever shoving our noses through the barbed wire at the roadside, while behind us endless acres of green pasture stretch away toward the blue horizon.

"Go everywhere," He says to us with a smile. "See after all things. Open all the rooms and look inside. Only keep out of this one room. Stay away from this one tree." And we stamp our feet, shake our fists, and demand to know why.

There's a very good reason why. It's the reason Bluebeard gave to his curious young wife just before setting out on his journey. It's the reason the Lord God gave to Adam and Eve when He put them in the garden and told them to enjoy themselves. If you enter this room, you will surely die. If you break down this fence and wander out onto this highway, you'll end up as road kill. If you touch this tree, something bad will happen. Your life is at stake. So pay attention.

Is that too much to ask?

Apparently so. The tragedy of human history is that day after day, year after year, generation after generation, and age after age, we insist on proving the validity of the prohibition by personal experience. Time after time we open the door, and time after time something dreadful ensues.

No wonder the songwriter asks, "When will they ever learn?" No wonder the storyteller crafts a tale that enshrines an echo of a memory, deep-seated within the soul of the race, that "all have sinned and fall short of the glory of God" (Romans 3:23). No wonder the mythmaker reminds us again and again that the results of failure in this area are severe and deadly: "For the wages of sin is death" (Romans 6:23).

If it's any consolation, the story of "Bluebeard" does have a happy ending. Although the returning husband, enraged at the discovery of his wife's disobedience, draws his sword and prepares to execute the sentence of death, the heroine's brothers arrive in time to rescue her. But that's no reason to discount the seriousness of the mistake she'd made.

In this case, curiosity may not have killed the cat. But it came awfully close.

# SAVAGE WORLD

## The Cruelty of Fallen Creation

"Hansel and Gretel" from the Brothers Grimm

*"I'll tell you what," answered his wife. "Early tomorrow*
*morning we'll take the children out into the forest*
*where it's most dense. We'll build a fire and give them*
*each a piece of bread. Then we'll go about our work*
*and leave them alone. They won't find their way*
*back home, and we'll be rid of them."*

I'm sick of waiting!" wheezed the horrid old hag. "*Sick*, I tell you! And I won't wait another day! Now fetch me some water and set it to boil!"

With the back of her scaly, withered hand, the bony old woman delivered a savage blow across Gretel's face. Her ear ringing, her jaw burning with pain, the poor girl stumbled backward and fell heavily against the wooden cage in which her brother, Hansel, was being held prisoner.

Gretel reached up and ran a fingertip along her cheek. She winced. Already a hot, stinging welt was rising between her earlobe and the corner of her mouth. Blood dribbled from her left nostril. Tears clouded her vision. A whimper pushed its way up from someplace deep down inside her chest.

That's when she felt it—the touch of a small hand on her

shoulder. She turned to see her brother's pale eyes gleaming at her from behind the rude wickerwork.

"Don't worry, Gretel," whispered Hansel. "There'll be some way out of this! There just *has* to be!"

But Gretel wasn't so sure. Her only response was a prayer. "Dear God, help us!" she breathed. "If only the wild beasts had eaten us in the forest! Then at least we could have died together!"

*Scrape. Scrape.* She watched in despair as the misshapen old crone dragged a huge black cauldron over to the hearth and hung it on the great hook over the fire. Struggling painfully to her feet, Gretel picked up two wooden buckets from a bench by the door and went out to fetch the water.

*If only the wild beasts had eaten us!* The thought passed through her mind once again as she lowered the first bucket into the well. It had nearly happened too; she and Hansel had had several narrow escapes with bears and wolves. After that, it was terror, darkness, and loneliness. Thirst and hunger, hunger and thirst. Two children alone at night in the middle of the great, dense Black Forest, deceived, betrayed, abandoned—by their own flesh and blood.

Not for the first time either. Oh no—though on that earlier occasion, Hansel had overheard their parents' plans as he lay awake, nursing his gnawing hunger pangs.

"Famine, husband!" their stepmother had hissed. "*Famine!* Do you understand what that means, you fool? We haven't enough to feed ourselves, let alone those two! I say we take them into the forest and lose them!"

Thanks to Hansel's cleverness, the children had managed to find their way home on that earlier occasion. But the boy's trick was too good to work twice. Breadcrumbs were a poor substitute for pebbles—the birds ate them up as soon as he dropped them, and the children searched in vain for the road home once dusk fell.

Approaching the cottage with buckets filled, Gretel bitterly recalled their first sight of the candle in the witch's marzipan-framed, sugar-paned window. It had looked so hopeful and inviting at the time.

"Fat or thin, thin or fat, I'll slaughter him anyway!" She could hear the nearsighted old biddy muttering and cackling to herself as she came in at the door. "Yes, slaughter him! And then eat him! I'll eat him *today!*"

With a grimace ugly as sin itself, the hag turned on Gretel, seized the two buckets, sloshed their contents into the kettle, and stoked the fire on the hearth until it was a roaring blaze. Then with her clawlike hand she grabbed the girl by the arm and thrust her out into the yard.

"Over there!" she screeched, pointing to the beehive-shaped oven that stood at the edge of the wood. "We have some baking to do!"

⚜

Though you won't find it in some of the sanitized versions lining the shelves of the children's section of the library, an unmistakable strain of sheer brutality runs through the traditional folk and fairy tales. It's frank and unapologetic, this element of violence and cruelty—naked and unadorned. Anyone even moderately familiar with the work of the Brothers Grimm, for instance, knows how truly grim the Grimms can be. Perhaps this is one of the reasons J. R. R. Tolkien suggested that fairy tales were never really meant for the nursery.[18] Their outlook on life is far too broad—and too realistic—for that.

"Hansel and Gretel," the perennial childhood favorite, provides a classic illustration of this more gruesome side of Fairy Land. Some of us have heard it so often we've grown numb to the horrors that lie at the heart of this tale—either that, or modern entertainment has numbed us to horror in general. Abandonment, abuse, and starvation; torture, death, and cannibalism—such are the bare facts of young Hansel and Gretel's daily lives. The few readers who haven't developed an immunity to the murder and mayhem of this story have probably toyed with the idea of circulating a petition to have the Brothers Grimm banned altogether. Either way, it's unlikely that many of us genuinely appreciate the story of "Hansel and Gretel" for what it is—and what it tells us about life in the real world.

For it reflects a vital and fundamental truth, this simple but shocking tale of two tender and innocent children who are left in the forest to die and only narrowly escape being turned into stew meat. Christians in particular have strong reasons to embrace, affirm, publish, and proclaim the message it conveys. For "Hansel and Gretel" reminds us that the world as we know it—a once-fair world now marred by the consequences of sin—is an extremely dangerous place. A *savage* place.

The tale of "Bluebeard," which we've already visited, communicates the same idea. So do many, many other fairy stories. Little Red Riding Hood faces the horrifying possibility of being eaten by a wolf, a possibility that is subsequently realized by her grandmother. Jack climbs a beanstalk only to hear that his bones may soon be ground to make the giant's bread. Little Tom Thumb must outwit a terrible ogre, who plans to eat him and his six brothers. Mr. Fox and the Robber Bridegroom lure young women to their luxurious country homes and then murder them in cold blood.

The most disturbing thing about all this is the hauntingly familiar ring to these tales. A contemporary ring. When it comes to violence and cruelty, many fairy tales read a bit too much like the daily newspapers. After all, what imaginary goblin or ghoul has ever inspired the kind of terror that Charles Manson and his crew actually inflicted upon the Tates and the La Biancas? How could Mr. Fox or the Robber Bridegroom ever hope to compete with the likes of Ted Bundy, who was responsible for the murder and mutilation of twenty-eight women and girls? What man-eating ogre ever presented a more appalling aspect to the world than the notorious Jeffrey Dahmer? What dark-eyed genie ever dealt out more death and destruction than the villainous Osama bin Laden?

The list goes on, of course. But the point here is not to terrify or titillate. Nor is it to echo the all-too-familiar alarmist message that society today is somehow worse than it's ever been. On the contrary, what "Hansel and Gretel" and the rest of the fairy tales teach us is that terror, cruelty, and savagery are simply "business as usual" in a tainted and fallen world. We shouldn't be surprised.

Neither should we be misled by the graphic extremism of the examples just cited. The dangers of this world can be subtle as well as overtly savage. Some of the most perilous are also the quietest, the most familiar, and the most inconspicuous. As the prophet Jeremiah saw so clearly, they're the goblins of the heart, for "the heart is deceitful above all things, and desperately wicked;

who can know it?" (Jeremiah 17:9). Fearsome are the ogres that dwell within: "fornication, uncleanness, passion, evil desire, and covetousness, which is idolatry" (Colossians 3:5).

What is it like to live in a world where, in spite of an over-abundance of superficial frills and material comforts, the inhabitants keep regular company with such demons? How does it feel to rub elbows on a daily basis with people "who, being past feeling, have given themselves over to lewdness, to work all uncleanness with greediness" (Ephesians 4:19)? What's it like to *be* those people? The answer is obvious. It's like sharing a cottage with a fang-toothed witch who has a taste for human flesh. It's like balancing yourself on the rim of a boiling cauldron.

Jesus warned His followers to expect trouble. "In the world," He said, "you will have tribulation" (John 16:33). He took for granted what many journalists and news commentators either never knew or have long since forgotten: that "the whole world lies under the sway of the wicked one" (1 John 5:19); that Satan, the great instigator of rebellion and the originator of self-worship and self-will, is, in fact, the very "god of this age" and the "ruler of this world" (2 Corinthians 4:4; John 14:30). Is it any surprise that the world is filled with deceit and bloodshed when its ruling spirit has been "a liar" and "a murderer from the beginning" (John 8:44)? Hansel and Gretel wouldn't have thought so.

Neither would the millions of believers who have known what it is to suffer injustice and cruelty at the enemy's hands. God's people are no strangers to the hostility, adversity, violence, and savagery that played such a prominent role in the adventures of Little Tom Thumb, Red Riding Hood, Snow White, the intrepid Jack, and those innocent babes in the woods, Hansel and Gretel. On the contrary,

> [Some] were tortured, not accepting deliverance, that they might obtain a better resurrection. Still others had trial of mockings and scourgings, yes, and of chains and imprisonment. They were stoned, they were sawn in two, were tempted, were slain with the sword. They wandered about in sheepskins and goatskins, being destitute, afflicted, tormented—of whom the world was not worthy. (Hebrews 11:35-38)

And yet in all these things, they were "more than conquerors" (Romans 8:37). Through all these afflictions, they earned by perseverance a deeper understanding of their Master's words: "Be of good cheer, I have overcome the world" (John 16:33). Ultimately, they proved that "savagery" is not the final word, and their story, like Hansel and Gretel's, had a gloriously happy ending.

# CREEPS AND SHIVERS

## *Wisdom and Fear*

"A Tale About the Boy Who Went Forth
to Learn What Fear Was"
from the Brothers Grimm

*At daybreak the boy put fifty talers in his pocket,*
*went out on a large highway, and kept saying to himself,*
*"If I could only get the creeps! If I could only get the creeps!"*

**I** *t's the oddest thing,* thought Martin as he sat, chin in hands, gazing into the glowing embers on the hearth. He breathed a sigh of discontent.

The cavernous fireplace was littered with ash and charred bones. The walls and paving stones at his feet were covered with suspicious-looking, ill-smelling stains. From above the massive stone mantelpiece, a blackened skull grinned down at him with an expression of malice, while just beside his ear a bulbous-bodied, glossy black spider dangled menacingly on an invisible thread. Ghostlike shreds of cobweb floated and fluttered on the icy drafts that swirled around his head and up into the murky shadows beneath the high-vaulted ceiling. But Martin didn't notice any of this. He was too busy thinking about what others had…and what he seemed so incapable of getting.

*The creeps. The shivers.*

His brother got them—at least he said he did. He got them whenever he walked through a graveyard at night. And his father said that they gripped him by the throat like a cold, clammy hand every time a black cat crossed his path. The neighbors claimed to tremble with them whenever the full moon rode the ragged clouds on Allhallow's Eve. But Martin? No. Not him. Not so much as a chill.

The townspeople talked, of course. "Never had the shivers," they muttered. "Ever met anyone like that?" His brother detested him. His father was ashamed. "Don't tell anyone where you come from or whose son you are." That was the last thing they had said as they pushed him out the door.

Martin scratched his head as one last little tongue of flame sputtered up among the coals. He *still* wanted to get them. That was the whole reason he'd left home in the first place. That's what had brought him to this isolated Transylvanian town. This dark, dank old castle was his last hope. It was supposed to be haunted.

"You'll get the creeps in there! No doubt about it!" the locals had assured him. "The king has promised his daughter to any man who can spend three nights inside. No one has ever come out alive!" But this was Martin's third night in the castle, and so far nothing had happened. Nothing he thought worth mentioning, at any rate.

As he reached for another log to throw on the fire, a piercing cry rent the dark air in the musty chamber.

"No need to raise your voice," yawned Martin, as down the chimney and out through the fireplace flew the half-decayed head of a rotting corpse. For a moment it hovered in the air just in front of him.

*"Aaaaahhhoooooiieeeee!"* howled the apparition, leering at Martin and blowing its foul breath straight into his face.

"Do you mind?" Martin was getting irritated. "I don't want your germs!" He took a backhanded swipe at the head and sent it flying through an open window. Then he stretched, lay down on the bench, and fell asleep.

Martin's new bride wasn't much happier with him than his father and brother had been.

"I never did get the shivers," he said glumly in answer to her rather pointed questions.

"Humph!" she said to herself. "If it's the shivers he wants, I believe I can accommodate him!"

That night, as soon as her young husband was asleep, she slipped out to the brook that ran through the castle garden. There she filled a bucket with icy water and a school of squirming little minnows. Returning to the palace, she stalked over to the bed and dumped the bucket's entire contents over Martin's head.

"Oh, joy!" he exclaimed, leaping to his feet in an ecstasy of sheer delight. "I've finally got them, dear wife! I've really, truly got the shivers at last!"

⚜

"He knows no fear," we say of someone we consider particularly bold or brave—someone like the Crocodile Hunter, or those heroic New York City firemen, or a diver who leaps unhesitatingly into the sea from the cliffs above Acapulco Bay. And we mean it as a compliment.

Not so in the case of the young man we'll call Martin, the fabled "Boy Who Went Forth to Learn What Fear Was." His is one of the oddest and most intriguing stories in the entire collection of the Brothers Grimm.

Martin's family, friends, and neighbors were fed up with his fearlessness. Too often they'd heard him complain about his inability to get "the creeps." So in a fit of exasperation they shipped him out to a place where they hoped he'd have ample opportunity to feel as many shivers as he pleased. But even in the land of vampires and werewolves, Martin simply couldn't get the hang of the horror thing.

What's this all about? The answer is simple: *comedy.* "The Boy Who Went Forth to Learn What Fear Was" is a fine example of the fairy-tale burlesque—a subgenre far more common in folklore than the uninitiated reader may suppose. It's a piece of drollery that creates its comic effect by posing a ridiculous what-if question—a device used ad absurdum by the early television sitcom writers. What if a horse could talk? What if a bunch of yokels from Appalachia moved to Beverly Hills? What if a man from Mars or the planet Ork came to live in your house? In this case the question is, "What if there really were such a thing as a person who had no fear?"

The answer, of course, is that this individual's life would be nothing but one long string of disaster, mishap, and buffoonery. Why? Because fear is essential to a safe, sane, and sensible life. That's why fearless Martin is portrayed not as a courageous hero, but as a ridiculous, pathetic, and pitiably defective human being. He's a clown, not a conqueror. His inability to get the creeps is funny precisely because it's so abnormal and unnatural.

Healthy fear fulfills a function similar to that of pain. It serves as a protection, a deterrent, a safeguard against the mortal dangers that surround us on every hand as we pick our way through the perilous maze of this savage world.

Physical pain, for all the discomfort and misery it causes, is actually a life-giving blessing. Victims of leprosy lose appendages and limbs precisely because they have no sensation of pain. "Pain," says Paul Brand, "…speaks to us as danger increases.… [It] shouts at us when the danger becomes severe: blisters, ulcers, and tissue damage break out, forcing us to change behavior."[19]

In the same way, fear can force us to change—or avoid—dangerous and damaging behaviors.

Are you scared of jumping off a ten-story building? You should be. Frightened to take a shortcut through a dark alley on the rough side of town? Consider yourself wise. Hesitant to get involved in an embezzlement scam? cheat on your spouse? ingest mind-altering drugs? Then get down on your knees and thank God for the marvelous gift of fear. Poor Martin would have given anything for a share in that blessing. A person who knows no such fear is either a fool or something worse. No wonder the book of Proverbs asserts, "How blessed is the man who fears always" (28:14, NASB).

This is not to deny, of course, that some kinds of fear can be unhealthy and harmful. Fear, to be helpful and constructive, must be rightly directed. Another way of saying this is that fear, like cholesterol, can be the good kind or the bad kind. Good fear negates and disarms the fear that debilitates and kills. And it's here that we come to the heart of the matter. For, like it or not, everybody has to fear somebody or something. To be like Martin, absolutely free of all fear whatsoever, is not only impossible; it's undesirable and dangerous.

Jesus sets the alternatives before us with crystalline clarity. "Do not fear those who kill the body but cannot kill the soul," He says.

> But rather fear Him who is able to destroy both soul and body in hell. Are not two sparrows sold for a copper coin? And yet not one of them falls to the ground apart from your Father's will. But the very hairs of your head are all numbered. Do not fear therefore; you are of more value than many sparrows. (Matthew 10:28-31)

A healthy, sober fear of God, who alone is able to "destroy both body and soul in hell" (Matthew 10:28), cancels out the fear of man and temporal circumstance. Only the wicked are devoid of this kind of fear—those people of whom Scripture says, "There is no fear of God before their eyes" (Romans 3:18).

> Therefore, my beloved, as you have always obeyed, not as in my presence only, but now much more in my absence, work out your own salvation with fear and trembling; for it is God who works in you both to will and to do for His good pleasure. (Philippians 2:12-13)

The message here is obvious: "Fear and trembling" are actually the flip side of trust. The truth of this assertion turns up again and again in the lives of the saints. For fear, great dread, and fits of doubt and despair have been characteristic of some of the greatest heroes of the faith. People like Jacob, who, after dreaming of angels and a stairway to heaven, awoke terrified and said, "How awesome is this place!" (Genesis 28:17). Or Moses, who, when directed to go down to Egypt and set his people free, stood quaking in his sandals and said, "Lord, please! Send someone else" (Exodus 4:13, NLT). Or Elijah, who immediately after his victory over the priests of Baal, fell into a deep depression and prayed, "Now, LORD, take my life, for I am no better than my fathers!" (1 Kings 19:4).

"If only I could get the creeps! If only I could get the creeps!" wailed poor hapless Martin. It might be a good thing if we all learned to pray a slightly revised version of his prayer, something like, "Oh, LORD;...unite my heart to fear Your name" (Psalm 86:11).

After all, "it is a fearful thing to fall into the hands of the living God" (Hebrews 10:31).

# EAST WIND, WEST WIND

## The Inscrutable Sovereignty of God

### "Mary Poppins" by P. L. Travers

*Michael gave a long sigh of relief. "That's all right,"*
*he said shakily. "She always does what she says she will."*

Hastily Jane tore away the brown wrapping paper and stood staring at the little painting. It was neatly set within a small, curly handmade frame. Underneath was an inscription: "Mary Poppins by Bert." A perfect likeness.

She blinked away the tears. Michael stood beside her, clutching the compass Mary Poppins had given him earlier that day. Jane could tell that he was watching her face—looking for some hint as to what it all meant, some sign of what was to come. Waiting for her to say something.

But Jane couldn't speak. She was too busy remembering. Remembering all the extraordinary and absolutely lovely things they had seen and done in the company of Mary Poppins. Thinking over the incredibly marvelous adventures they'd been having ever since that raw autumn day when she first banged up against the gate at Number Seventeen Cherry Tree Lane.

She thought about her very first sight of the new nanny: a spare-limbed, plain-faced, black-haired woman in dark clothes, holding her hat on with one hand and carrying a large bag in the other. She recalled the newcomer's brief, authoritative manner in responding to Mrs. Banks's inquiry about references—"Oh, I make it a rule never to give them"—and the short, severe, no-nonsense tone with which she at once took her new charges in hand—"Spit-spot into bed! One more word from that direction and I'll call the Policeman!"

Jane could hardly keep back a smile as she pictured to herself the marvels of Mary Poppins's first evening in the house: how she slid *up* the banisters; how the entirety of her worldly possessions, including a folding armchair and a camp bed, came out of what appeared to be an empty carpetbag; how the "medicine" in her bottle changed color and flavor to suit the patient's personal taste. She heard again the words Michael had spoken before getting into bed that night: "Mary Poppins, you'll never leave us, will you?"

But she *had* left them. Staring down at the painting, Jane tried to take it in.

"I'll stay till the wind changes." That had been her promise, and she had kept it. Jane saw this clearly now. Thinking it over, she realized that the wind had been in the west since early that morning. The wind had shifted, and Mary Poppins had gone away: over the rooftops and the cherry trees, beyond the park, over the hill, and up into the cloudy air, her open umbrella in one hand, carpetbag in the other.

How could she do it? How *could* she go—after all they'd been through together? After the Bird Woman and the Dancing Cow? After the tea party on the ceiling and the midnight revels at the zoo (both of which she vehemently denied)? After Fannie and Annie and Mrs. Corry's gingerbread? It was simply too devastating. How could life go on without her? "Mary Poppins is the only person I want in the world!" Michael had wailed. Jane felt the same way.

She was about to lay a comforting hand on her brother's shoulder when suddenly she noticed something that had previously escaped her attention. There was a note attached to the painting!

Dear Jane,

Michael had the compass so the picture is for you.
Au revoir.

Mary Poppins

"Au revoir," she read in a whisper. "Mrs. Brill!" she called. "What does *au revoir* mean?"

"Au revore, dearie?" blustered the housekeeper. "Why, doesn't it mean 'God bless you'? No. No, I'm wrong. I think it means 'to meet again.'"

Jane and Michael turned to one another with shining eyes.

They knew what Mary Poppins meant.

⚜

Just who *is* this Poppins person? We can almost hear Mr. Banks, red faced and hyperventilating, demanding an answer from his patient wife and bewildered household staff. Many of us would like to know too.

But for Jane and Michael Banks—and the millions of children

who have followed their adventures with Mary since the first Poppins book appeared in 1934—the more important question has always been, "When is she coming back?" Can anybody blame them?

Given author P. L. Travers's personal affinities for mysticism and spiritualism, it's anybody's guess what she had in mind when the unforgettable English nanny first began to take shape beneath her pen. But one thing's certain: In Mary Poppins, Travers has given us a literary personality of peculiar power and rare winsomeness. Anyone who reads as far as the final chapter will have no trouble understanding why Michael reacts so violently to the thought of engaging a new nanny. There could never be another like her.

Bear in mind that we're talking here about the real Mary Poppins—not the lovely Julie Andrews. We're referring to the Mary whose hair is as black and shiny as a wooden Dutch doll's, who wears funny flowered hats, and whose hands and feet look disproportionately large at the ends of her thin and spindly arms and legs. Plain-faced, pointy-nosed Mary, whose manner with the children is generally described as "cross." Haughty, aloof, imperious Mary, who sniffs more often than she speaks, who never explains anything, and who tolerates nonsense from nobody. Why do readers love her? Why does Michael weep and wail to have her back?

A great deal of the answer lies in the quirks and oddities themselves. Clearly, Mary Poppins is no ordinary nanny.

What manner of woman is this who understands and interprets the speech of animals and birds? Who sends you on a trip around the world with a mere flick of the compass needle? Who changes strawberry ice into a lime-juice cordial with a wink of her eye? One might well ask. For Mary Poppins's talents and abilities extend far beyond the mere production of campstools from carpetbags. She comes and goes with the shifting of the winds. She defies the normal limitations of gravity, space, and time. She climbs a ladder and hangs the stars in the sky. She opens her umbrella and ascends into the clouds. She's that sort of person.

Michael discovered this at his very first meeting with the new mistress of the nursery. He found that it was impossible to look Mary Poppins in the eye and disobey her. To his surprise and delight, he realized that there was something altogether extraordinary about this particular nanny, "something that was frightening and at the same time most exciting."[20]

Mrs. Banks ran into the same thing during her initial interview with the applicant for Katie Nanna's recently vacated post. By the time a decision had been reached, it was abundantly clear who was *really* in control. For Mary had a maddening way of stepping in and taking charge. What's more, she accomplished this with such diplomacy and aplomb that everyone ended up feeling happy and relieved about it. They couldn't imagine how they had ever managed without her.

Herein lies the secret of Mary's intoxicating charm, the key to her irresistible mystique: She meets people and circumstances purely on her own terms. Down wild and wandering pathways she guides her bright-eyed young charges, dishing up marvels and miracles every step of the way, never offering a word of justification for her strange habits, impenetrable moods, and incomprehensible methods. She is completely, if inexplicably, in charge. And the outcome of her eccentric and beneficent tyranny is, without fail, something incontestably good so that everyone in the household, including the testy and irritable Mr. Banks, ends up being glad of her coming. Whether she shares their positive assessment of the situation is, of course, another matter, for Mary never tells anybody anything.

Can we encounter the delightfully enigmatic Mary Poppins without being reminded of the Carpenter from Nazareth, of whom the apostle John writes that He "did not commit Himself to them, because He knew all men" (John 2:24)? Jesus, too, spoke in conundrums and riddles. He regularly couched His teaching in opaque parables, "lest they should see with their eyes and hear with their ears" (Matthew 13:15). It's no wonder that C. S. Lewis refers to Christ as the most elusive of teachers: "Systems cannot keep up with that darting illumination. No net less wide than a man's whole heart, nor less fine of mesh than love, will hold the sacred Fish."[21] He might have been talking about Mary Poppins.

Though this probably wasn't Travers's intention, it is possible to see in her story of the inscrutable nanny a parable of our inscrutable God. For He, too, has something about Him that is "frightening and at the same time most exciting." Like the nanny at Number Seventeen Cherry Tree Lane, His work in our lives is as uncontrollable and as powerful as the wind:

> As you do not know what is the way of the wind,
> Or how the bones grow in the womb of her who is with
>        child,
> So you do not know the works of God who makes every-
>        thing. (Ecclesiastes 11:5)

The wind blows where it wishes, and you hear the sound
of it, but cannot tell where it comes from and where it
goes. So is everyone who is born of the Spirit. (John 3:8)

We will love this untamable God desperately, just as the
Banks children loved Mary Poppins, when we come to understand that He is not merely wild and unpredictable but also
utterly faithful and reliable—that He always does what He says
He will.

I am God, and there is none like Me,
Declaring the end from the beginning,
And from ancient times things that are not yet done,
Saying, "My counsel shall stand,
And I will do all My pleasure." (Isaiah 46:9-10)

The implication is obvious. If, in His parting message, Christ
has given us His *au revoir,* we may be certain that the time is coming when we will, indeed, "meet again."

Just wait. The sequel is coming.

# Divine Monstrosity

## The Lover Behind the Gruesome Mask

"Beauty and the Beast"
by Jeanne-Marie LePrince de Beaumont

*"No, dear Beast!" said Beauty. "You must not die!
Live to be my husband; from this moment I give you my hand
and swear to be none but yours. Alas! I thought I had
only a friendship for you, but the grief I now feel
convinces me that I cannot live without you."*

She woke in a cold sweat and sat bolt upright among the pillows, staring wildly into the darkness. What had she been dreaming?

Pulling the coverlet aside, she swung her feet out of bed and stole softly to the window. Outside the light was growing in the sky. She sat down on the sill and leaned her forehead against the glass.

It was all coming back to her now: Beast, stretched full length upon the grass beside his garden pond; Beast, wheezing in his death throes, breathing out words of blame and reproach against her. Poor, horrible, ugly, brutish Beast, dying for want of his Beauty.

*How could I lie to him?* she thought. *How could I be so cruel? Can he help it that he is so dreadfully misshapen?* She put her head in her hands and squeezed her eyes tightly shut.

"Belle! My Little Beauty!" Her father's cheerful voice rang out in the passage. "Are you up?"

She rose; quietly she crossed to the door. "Yes, Papa," she said, opening to him with a tired smile. "Yes, I am awake."

"It is so good," the old man cried, hugging her neck, "so *good* to have you home again!"

Gratefully she stroked his thinning gray hair and blinked back a weary tear. Nine days she had been in her father's house— nine whole days, in spite of her promise to return to Beast in seven. "You need only lay this ring on a table before you go to bed," the monster had told her on the eve of her departure, "when you have a mind to come back."

But she had no mind to go back. That's what she told herself, over and over again, all throughout that day. But the nightmare lingered in her brain. Nothing—not the joy of her father's company, not the fellowship of his table, not the delights of a walk in his garden—would drive it from her.

That night she sat on the edge of her bed, twisting the little gold ring around and around on her finger. Go back to him? The very idea repulsed her. Go back and become his bride? He had been gentle with her, yes, but he was, after all, a beast. Go back and marry a beast? She shuddered at the thought. She trembled, picturing his horrid red maw and his knifelike claws smoking with the blood of the prey he caught in the woods beyond his courtyard walls. Again she heard the gurgle in the monster's throat as he timidly put the question to her: "Beauty, will you be my wife?"

*No.* It was unthinkable! It was simply too horrible and night-marish to be real! She would not leave her father again! She could not marry an animal, however gentle and kind. She pressed her hands to her temples and closed her eyes. She bit her lip, tore her hair, and gnashed her teeth.

Then she took off the ring, laid it on the table, and plunged beneath the bedcovers.


Waking in Beast's palace, Beauty leapt out of bed, her heart pounding. Quickly she threw open the door and rushed out into the garden.

He was lying beside the pond when she found him…just as she had seen him in her dream. Reeling under the force of her own emotions, she fell upon his prostrate form, kissed his furred cheek profusely, and burst out weeping.

"You must not die, dear Beast!" she cried. "Until this moment I did not realize it, but now I know it all too well! I cannot live without you!"

A flash of lightning. A rumble of thunder. Opening one eye, she saw the whole palace sparkling as if with fireworks. What could it be? She raised herself on one elbow, glanced down at him…and gasped.

For there he lay, smiling rosily up at her from the ground— the handsomest, most radiant young prince in the world.

❧

"A great good is coming—is coming—is coming to thee, Anodos," says a voice at the conclusion of George MacDonald's *Phantastes*.

And so it is. A great good is coming to all of us. The sad thing is that so few recognize and embrace it when it arrives.

Not that this is difficult to understand. The good that comes our way often passes undetected because it presents itself in such strange and unexpected forms. It assumes the shape of a monster. It frightens us by leaping out, apparition-like, from a closet or a back alley. It sneaks up on us in disguise. "Unfair!" we shout. "Tricky!" And in a certain sense we're right. Nevertheless, that's often the way it works. Especially in the realm of the Spirit.

Beauty entered the house of the Beast in terror, believing that she was going forth to her death. What else was she to think? Beast had threatened to kill her father for plucking a rose in his garden. When he discovered that the poor man had daughters, he said, "I will forgive you on condition that one of them come willingly and suffer for you." So Beauty went. She went like a lamb to the slaughter, out of pure, unselfish love. She went fully expecting to die in her father's place. She hadn't the faintest premonition of the great good that was coming her way.

Beauty's position at this point is not unlike that of the patriarch Job. He, too, was confronted with a horror so huge, so overwhelming, so incomprehensible that he simply could not wrap his mind around it. He lost everything: his children, his wealth, his flocks, his herds, his health. Though Job fought hard to hold on to his integrity and his love for God, it was difficult under the circumstances to see the Lord as anything but a complete monster. How *could* he accept his lot as a gift from the Lover of his soul?

The arrows of the Almighty are within me;
My spirit drinks in their poison;

The terrors of God are arrayed against me.
Does the wild donkey bray when it has grass,
Or does the ox low over its fodder?
Can flavorless food be eaten without salt?
Or is there any taste in the white of an egg?
My soul refuses to touch them;
They are as loathsome food to me. (Job 6:4-7)

*Loathsome.* That's exactly how Beauty felt about the Beast.
That's why, when the monster offered her an opportunity to go
home and visit her father, she jumped at the chance. And when
it was time to return, she procrastinated and made excuses.

Many of us have had a similar experience, though the
specifics vary. The loss of a job. The death of a spouse or child.
The failure of a dream. Financial collapse. Betrayal at the hands
of a friend. All at once God begins to look very much like a beast.
So we shudder and withdraw. We retreat to scrape our sores, lick
our wounds, and nurse our bitterness and resentment. Respect
Him as Lord of the universe? Perhaps. Worship Him as the
Sovereign Ruler of all? Maybe. But embrace Him as Husband
and Lover? Never. Not a God who could allow *that* to happen.
Such a God is far too monstrous and ugly.

So why did Beauty go back? If you had asked her at the time,
she probably couldn't have explained it. She didn't know herself.
In the beginning it was purely a matter of duty. She acted out of
a confused and anguished mixture of feelings simply because it
seemed the right thing to do. But by the time she stood in the
garden above the body of the expiring Beast, she had come to a
shocking realization: She loved the monster—loved him in spite

of his ugliness and her revulsion. More than that, she knew that she couldn't live without him.

That's when Beauty's "great good" came crashing in on her like a clap of thunder out of a summer-blue sky. At that very moment, and not a second sooner, it was revealed to her that Beast was not a beast at all, but a gloriously handsome, utterly desirable young prince, a prince to whom she could devote herself with all her heart, soul, mind, and strength. Contrary to all expectation, her terrible doom turned out to be the best thing that could have happened to her.

Job came to a similar place of enlightenment:

> I have uttered what I did not understand,
> Things too wonderful for me, which I did not know....
> I have heard of You by the hearing of the ear,
> But now my eye sees You.
> Therefore I abhor myself,
> And repent in dust and ashes. (Job 42:3,5-6)

At this point Job's pain and abject humiliation were transformed into contentment and delight. His sorrow became joy. And the denouement was that "the LORD blessed the latter days of Job more than his beginning" (Job 42:12).

"Truly You are God, who hide Yourself, O God of Israel, the Savior!" complains the prophet (Isaiah 45:15). The psalmist agrees: "Clouds and darkness surround Him!" (Psalm 97:2). Some of us know exactly what they mean. God has concealed Himself from us behind clouds of misfortune, anguish, and pain.

He has crept back into a dark corner and then leaped out wearing a hideous mask.

But the day is coming when we, like Beauty, will pierce that frightening facade. The loveliness that hides behind the horror will emerge at last when we realize that this monstrous, hidden God is, in fact, the only Lover fit to be the Husband of our souls—that, in spite of everything, we cannot live without Him.

> Whom have I in heaven but You?
> And there is none upon earth that I desire besides You.
> My flesh and my heart fail;
> But God is the strength of my heart and my portion
>          forever. (Psalm 73:25-26)

Lay the ring on the table. It's time to go back. A great good is coming to *you*.

# SEEKING LOVE

*God's Relentless Grace*

"The Snow Queen" by Hans Christian Andersen

*She stepped into the vast empty cold halls—*
*then she saw Kay, she recognized him, she flung herself*
*about his neck, held him very tight, and cried,*
*"Kay! Dear little Kay! So I've found you after all!"*

The driving snow stung her eyes. The wind cut like a polished blade. Shielding her face with one arm, Gerda stepped out from behind the shelter of a frozen gorse bush and pushed on across the blinding white waste.

Little Kay! How she missed him! The sharp prick of the ice and snow against her bare skin was as nothing compared to the pain of losing her friend.

*He is not dead!* she told herself as she forged ahead against the impossible wind and weather of northernmost Finmark. She could not, would not believe it! No matter what they said, she would search for Kay until she found him. She would do anything, go anywhere, suffer any amount of hardship and pain, if only she might bring him home again.

Overcome with loneliness, Gerda began to cry, the tears freezing solid on her cheeks. Thinking of the terrible changes that had come over Kay just prior to his disappearance, she realized that, while he might not be dead, Kay was surely altered—dreadfully, fearfully altered. He had become cold and calculating, devoid of feeling, his heart like a lump of ice. She had seen it in his eyes and in his actions, in the cruel and callous words with which he had taunted her the last time they were together. He had hurt her terribly, but it didn't matter. Her feelings for him hadn't changed. Somehow, she had to save him from himself…and from the deadly chilling enchantments of the Snow Queen.

The Snow Queen. She had swept through the town and stolen Kay away in her great white sledge. After that, she had hidden him deep inside her frigid arctic fortress under the northern lights. Gerda knew this; the old Finnish woman had told her so. "He is with the Snow Queen right enough," she said. "He's got a splinter of glass in his heart and a little grain of it in his eye. And unless you can get them out, he'll never be human again."

All at once the wind dropped. Gerda looked up. She was standing before a series of mountainous blue-white snowdrifts— the walls of the Snow Queen's palace! Her heart leaped for joy… and then fell into despair and fear. What if she found him but he refused to go with her? What if the splinter and grain of glass would not come out of his heart and eye? What if they both died of the cold before they were able to escape?

But it was no use asking such questions. The only thing that counted now was Gerda's love for Kay. Trembling with cold and fear, she approached the door and stepped over the crystal threshold. For a moment she stood gaping up into the awful empty vastness of the Snow Queen's halls, staring at the cavernous ceilings, the glassy stalactites, and the massive ice pillars illuminated by the cold flashes of the aurora borealis.

Suddenly she caught sight of him—little Kay! He was sitting far out in the middle of a cracked, frozen lake that lay in the very center of the palace, playing with shards of shattered ice as if they were the pieces of a Chinese puzzle. His skin was as blue as his eyes, and a blank, uncomprehending look dominated his stiff, frozen face.

She ran to him. She hugged him. He moved not a muscle but continued staring straight ahead.

"Kay! Dear Kay!" she cried. But still he sat motionless, as if frozen to death.

At that moment Gerda's heart broke. She fell on his neck and wept hot tears, tears that fell upon Kay's breast and penetrated his heart. Then she began to sing the old hymn they had so often sung together beneath the rose trees on the rooftop back at home.

In the valley grew roses wild,
And there we spoke with the Holy Child![22]

All at once something seemed to snap inside of Kay. He, too, burst into tears. So desperately and profusely did he weep that the grain of glass was washed out of his eye.

"Gerda!" he cried, looking up and recognizing her at last. "Where did *you* come from? And why is it so cold here?"

⚜

What would you do if the friend and companion of your child-hood, the sharer of your deepest secrets, the custodian of the keys to your heart, suddenly became a stranger? What if he or she laughed in your face, spit upon your most cherished ideals, and dashed your hopes and dreams to the ground? What if you knew beyond a shadow of a doubt that this person no longer had even the slightest regard for your feelings?

That's what Kay had done to Gerda. At least that's how she felt about it in the beginning. Only much later did she learn the full truth: that it was the Snow Queen's irresistible allurements and enchantments that had taken the boy captive and caused him to treat his friend with such disdain. This knowledge came to Gerda only after she had already taken up the quest to find her soul mate and win him back at any cost…in spite of the pain he'd caused her.

Those three little words—*in spite of*—are the operative phrase here. Clearly, it's what Gerda didn't know that made all the difference. If she had understood the truth, her search for Kay, though still admirable and heroic, would affect us quite differently. It would strike us as being merely logical—precisely what we would expect between faithful, dedicated, lifelong friends. But Gerda sought Kay after he had rejected her and before she knew the deeper reason for his bizarre Jekyll-and-Hyde transformation. She traveled all the way to the heart of darkness in an effort to regain the wayward companion of her childhood. In so doing, she became for us a model of seeking love.

Seeking love. Pursuing love. Love that continues relentlessly in spite of rejection and pain. The scriptures of the Old and New Testaments sing to us constantly of such a love. It is, in fact, their central theme from beginning to end.

Didn't the Lord God love Adam and Eve in just this way when He came looking for them in the garden in the cool of the day? When, to entice them from their hiding places, He gently called out, "Adam! Where are you?" Surely He must have known how they had disobeyed Him and disregarded His Word! Why, then, did He bother to search them out and engage them in dialogue? Why not simply blast them off the face of the earth? Hadn't He said, "In the day that you eat of it [the tree of the knowledge of good and evil] you shall surely die" (Genesis 2:17)?

And didn't He paint a similar picture of His undying love for a stiff-necked people when He instructed Hosea to take back his wanton wife? "Go again," He said to the prophet, "love a woman who is loved by a lover and is committing adultery, just like the love of the LORD for the children of Israel" (Hosea 3:1). Later on in Hosea's prophecy, God expresses His love for His incorrigible children in even more poignant terms:

> How can I give you up, Ephraim?
> How can I hand you over, Israel?
> How can I make you like Admah?
> How can I set you like Zeboiim?
> My heart churns within Me;
> My sympathy is stirred.
> I will not execute the fierceness of my anger.
>     (Hosea 11:8-9)

The love of God is resilient and elastic beyond belief. It stretches itself across barriers of sin and over mountains of offense. It pinpoints and pursues, corners and captures even those renegades who have thumbed their noses in their Maker's face. It runs to meet those who have tossed it aside and discounted its

worth—as in Jesus' famous parable about a father and his prodi-
gal son:

> But when he was still a great way off, his father saw him
> and had compassion, and ran and fell on his neck and
> kissed him....
>
> [And] the father said to his servants, "Bring out the best
> robe and put it on him, and put a ring on his hand and
> sandals on his feet. And bring the fatted calf here and kill it,
> and let us eat and be merry; for this my son was dead and is
> alive again; he was lost and is found." (Luke 15:20,22-24)

"Wise men still seek Him," reads the Yuletide bumper sticker.
But the deeper truth is that He seeks us, just as a shepherd seeks
his lost sheep or a housewife her lost coin (Luke 15:4-10). His
love for us is a hounding, harrying love, a love that never gives up.
There is no hiding from His ever-searching, never-resting eye:

> Where can I go from Your Spirit?
> Or where can I flee from Your presence?
> If I ascend into heaven, You are there;
> If I make my bed in hell, behold, You are there.
> If I take the wings of the morning,
> And dwell in the uttermost parts of the sea,
> Even there Your hand shall lead me,
> And Your right hand shall hold me. (Psalm 139:7-10)

The poet Francis Thompson, a man who squandered much
of the vigor of his youth in an attempt to flee from that pursuing

love, later wrote about his flight and the "strong Feet that followed, followed after":

> With unhurrying chase,
>     And unperturbèd pace,
> Deliberate speed, majestic instancy,
>     They beat—and a Voice beat
>     More instant than the Feet—
> "All things betray thee, who betrayest Me."[23]

Happily, Thompson came to a good end. Like Andersen's little Kay, this fugitive was eventually caught—apprehended and taken into custody. And he lived to confess that no happier fate awaits any man or woman on earth than to be pursued, captured, and possessed by the Love that never falters and never abandons the chase.

> Halts by me that footfall:
>     Is my gloom, after all,
> Shade of His hand, outstretched caressingly?
>     "Ah, fondest, blindest, weakest,
>     I am He Whom thou seekest!
> Thou dravest love from thee, who dravest Me."[24]

# Impossible Odds

## The Miracle of Mercy

### "The Red Shoes" by Hans Christian Andersen

*When they had finished the hymn and looked up,*
*they nodded and said, "It was right of you to come, Karen."*
*"It was mercy," said she.*

Karen sat on the hard little wooden chair, her gaze fixed upon the Bible that lay open on her knees. Her prosthetic wooden feet clacked together with a dull, dead sound as she shifted her weight. Her vision blurred. Wiping her eyes, she stared up at the blank plaster wall of the tiny garret room. Who would have thought that such a pretty little girl should have come to such a dismal end!

Through the wall, dim and distant, came the sounds of hymn singing. Insistently, persistently, they seeped into the parsonage from the church next door. The kind pastor and his wife and children had begged her to accompany them to the service. But Karen had quietly demurred. She would pray her prayers alone, she said, and finish the housework. How could she possibly go?

Not that she hadn't tried. She had—more than once. But it was always the same. Every time she approached the church door, they were there. Dancing on the threshold. Taunting and terrifying her, flitting this way and that in a scarlet shimmer, capering demonically before her eyes in a hellish display of mockery and derision.

*The Red Shoes.*

Karen had been warned, of course. The benevolent old woman who adopted her as an orphaned urchin had said it over and over again. "Not the Red Shoes, dear. You mustn't wear them. They are shocking and improper." But once her heart was set on them, Karen could not get the Red Shoes out of her mind.

How frightened she was to discover that they would not come off her feet either! She tried to stop dancing but could not control her legs! Though she screamed and wept, she could not still the wild flailing of her own body nor pry the horrid blood-red shoes away from her flesh. Away they danced with her, through the dark woods and over the lonely moors. Never once did they give her a moment's rest, until at last she was driven to the house of the executioner with a desperate, unthinkable plea on her lips: "Cut off my feet!"

And now? Now she sat in the little garret, staring through tears at the crutches in the corner. The pastor and his family had been unfailingly good to her ever since she came to their door seeking work and a place to stay. They genuinely loved her, and she loved them dearly in return. But even now she was not free. Even now she dared not take a step outside for fear of the Red Shoes.

But wait! The sounds of singing were growing louder. Karen looked up in astonishment. Was it possible? The walls of her narrow little room were swinging open! A blinding light was streaming in through the breach. And now an angel was standing before her, shining like the sun. She saw him reach up and touch the ceiling with a spray of red roses. Immediately a brilliant golden star appeared above his head. In the next moment, ceiling and walls vanished altogether, the organ notes trumpeted forth, and Karen suddenly found herself sitting beside the pastor's family at the front of the church.

Utterly bewildered by this inexplicable change in her surroundings, she turned and stared at the faces of the singing parishioners in the pews behind her. Out of their mouths poured golden words—words that made her feel like a newborn babe:

> Thine eye diffused a quick'ning ray;
> I woke—the dungeon flamed with light!
> My chains fell off, my heart was free,
> I rose, went forth, and followed Thee.[25]

The pastor's wife leaned over and touched her arm. "It was right of you to come, Karen," she said with a smile.

Karen, still at a blissful loss, smiled meekly in return.

"It was mercy," she said.

⚜

"If you know these things," said Jesus, "blessed are you if you do them" (John 13:17).

But what if you can't? Such a certainty paralyzes too many of us all too often.

Contrary to the popular maxim, knowledge is not necessarily power—at least not in the moral and spiritual realm. It's entirely possible to have a full and competent grasp of right and wrong yet find yourself not only unwilling but unable to choose the good. The apostle Paul experienced this dilemma a long time ago: "What I am doing, I do not understand. For what I will to do, that I do not practice; but what I hate, that I do" (Romans 7:15).

Paul knew what it was like to be up against impossible odds. He looked within himself and proved by personal experience the daunting truth of the psalmist's complaint: "There is none who does good, no, not one" (Psalm 53:3).

"Can the Ethiopian change his skin or the leopard its spots?" asked Jeremiah. The answer, of course, is *no*. It's impossible. "Then may you also do good," concluded the prophet, "who are accustomed to do evil" (Jeremiah 13:23). Not a terribly encouraging picture.

Hans Christian Andersen's Karen is not the only hapless heroine ever to find herself slammed up against the wall of her own inability. Impossible odds are a familiar part of the drama of fairy stories.

Just put yourself in the place of that unfortunate maiden whose father, a poor but opportunistic miller, decided to pad his chances for social advancement with this harmless little white lie: "I have a daughter who can spin straw into gold!" Picture yourself locked inside a huge, echoing, high-ceilinged stone chamber with nothing but a spinning wheel and bales upon bales of pale yellow straw. Imagine the sound of the door shutting you in, the click of the lock, and the voice of the king shouting through the grate: "Now get to work! If you don't spin this straw into gold by morning, then you must die!"

Spiritually speaking, we all know what it's like to be up against impossible odds. We who have so often been beaten up and held down by our own fallibility and the power of indwelling sin can't help but hear the sound of dancing Red Shoes in the ring of Jesus' uncompromising words: "Therefore, you shall be perfect, just as your Father in heaven is perfect" (Matthew 5:48); "For I say to you, that unless your righteousness exceeds the righteousness of the scribes and Pharisees, you will by no means enter the kingdom of heaven" (Matthew 5:20).

That's why it's altogether conceivable that men and women who are fully convinced of God's reality, goodness, and love will nevertheless hang back when it comes to committing themselves unreservedly to His care. They'd like to, but they can't. An invisible barrier, unbreachable as China's Great Wall, is somehow blocking the way.

Some are gripped by this paralysis at the first instant of hearing God's call. They know that He is inviting them to come home, and their hearts ache to respond. But no sooner have they taken a step toward His house than they are greeted by a daunting apparition: the Red Shoes, dancing on the threshold, leaping and gamboling before their eyes like the flames of hell itself. Past mistakes, present indiscretions, all those inescapable follies and sins—the things they thought they had left behind, but which cling to them nevertheless like horrid cobwebs. The whole sorry mess positions itself there in the doorway like a grim, ghostly policeman, blocking their entrance and barring the door.

Others of us have fought this battle—fought and *lost*—so many times that we've decided to throw in the towel. Like Karen, we feel shut in, closed off, excluded, or cut off from God and the streams of eternal life. We sit, crippled, in our narrow little rooms, listening to the songs outside, staring bleary-eyed at the pages of

Scripture, finding its promises lifeless and gray. We'd like to believe like the rest of them. We're desperate to rise up and walk, to live out the implications of a vibrant faith. But we can't. We know ourselves too well. We've failed too many times to try again.

Perhaps, like Karen, some of us have even taken the words of Christ to heart: "If your right eye causes you to sin, pluck it out and cast it from you.… And if your right hand causes you to sin, cut it off and cast it from you" (Matthew 5:29-30). At great cost, we have performed radical surgery upon ourselves. We have endured the pain of cutting off undesirable associations, of excising destructive habits, attitudes, and activities from our lives. We've done everything we thought we were supposed to do. We've repented in the true sense of the word. And still we can't get past this abominable wall.

"O wretched man that I am!" cried Paul when he found himself in this position. "Who will deliver me from this body of death?" (Romans 7:24).

For the apostle, as for Karen, the answer comes in an unexpected flash. It's not a matter of increased knowledge or improved education. Nor is it the result of untiring efforts to "do the right thing." It's more in the nature of an epiphany—a deliverance that can only be described as a sudden, supernatural gift.

The walls open out, and the ceiling comes off. The hand of God reaches in, lifts us out of our personal prison, and brings us to rest in the heart of His love. We look around and find that, somehow or other, the impossible has been accomplished. We're not sure how it happened. All we know is that we're glad to be there. With Paul, we change the cry of our heart from "Woe is me!" to "Thanks be to God through Jesus Christ our Lord!"

(Romans 7:25, NASB). With all the childish wonder of a young girl in the presence of a mighty angel, we suddenly realize the joyous inescapability of that other uncompromising declaration of Jesus: "With men this is impossible, but with God all things are possible" (Matthew 19:26).

Someone turns and says, "You did the right thing by coming."

And like Karen, we smile and answer, "I didn't do anything at all. It was mercy."

# GOLDEN TRUMPET

*Free in Christ*

"Jack the Giant-Killer," an English folk tale

> *Whoever shall this trumpet blow,*
> *Shall soon the giant overthrow,*
> *And break the black enchantment straight;*
> *So all shall be in happy state.*

Raising her soft brown eyes, she cast a despairing look up at
the impassable stone rampart that encircled the courtyard.
A tear trembled at the end of one dark eyelash, then fell and
splashed off a cloven black hoof.

Once upon a time she had been the daughter of a duke, a
young duchess of incontestable beauty and grace. Every day she
wore silk and cashmere and rustling damask. Her feet had been
shod in fair slippers of white satin embroidered with thread of
spun gold.

But now she was a prisoner. A prisoner of the giant. And
though, even in captivity, she retained traces of her former beauty,
it was no longer the beauty of a nobleman's daughter. It was not,
in fact, the beauty of a maiden at all.

It was the beauty of a doe—a three-year-old white hind.

Try as she might, she could not recall exactly how it had happened. Now and again, as she stared down at her cloven feet,

snatches of a remembered walk in the garden would flash through her mind. Images of a storm, of wind and fire. A struggle. A face as big and as broad as the moon, distorted and blotched. A hard, cruel laugh. And then the huge hand of her captor, the giant Galligantua, blotting out the light.

She had come to herself in this dismal gray courtyard, in the company of a multitude of beasts, birds, and crawling things. Here lived rabbits and horses, antelope and deer, ravens and doves, snakes and toads—every sort of creature imaginable, each with the same shattered look of loss and utter despair in its eyes.

It was an enchantment, of course. She knew that. She knew that these beasts were not beasts at all but maidens like herself and young knights and noblemen, all of them kidnapped, carried away, and cast under the giant's spell.

She knew it because the giant himself bragged about it incessantly. He was boasting about his feats now, standing on the steps of the castle and browbeating the helpless creatures with the hopelessness of their position, telling them for the thousandth time that, though many brave knights and heroes had tried, none had been able to breach his walls or break the enchantment.

"It's too bad!" he mocked. "For if a man could only reach the gate, the game would be up! All he'd have to do is blow the golden trumpet that hangs there. But no one can do it! No one can get past my terrible, sharp-clawed griffins! No one can—"

He stopped in midsentence. For at that moment a high, clear note rang out from someplace just beyond the courtyard wall. The young doe saw the giant's face turn pale.

Again that pure clarion call! And then a rumbling, a trembling as of the castle's very foundations. *Can it be true?* Her heart was fluttering like a leaf. *Is the spell really breaking?*

The courtyard walls began to shake and totter. Stones fell to the ground, raising huge clouds of dust. On every side the young doe saw animals leaping and jumping, in fear and excitement dashing themselves against the rocks, hiding their heads behind piles of rubble. Then from out of nowhere flashed a bright blade. Off flew the giant's head! A whirlwind spiraled to the ground and swept his loathsome corpse into the air. In the next instant the whole castle vanished in a cloud of smoke.

As the smoke and dust cleared, she caught sight of her own two feet. They were shod in slippers of white satin. A black cloak swept through the air before her eyes, and an odd figure emerged from behind it—a young man, barely more than a boy, with a crop of disheveled black hair sticking out from under his rumpled cap. He held a sharp sword in his hand, and a pair of outlandish, curly toed shoes adorned his feet. Around his waist he wore a leather belt, and on the belt, embroidered in letters of gold, were these words:

Here's the right valiant Cornish man
Who slew the giant Cormoran.[76]

"Sorry!" he said, stumbling forward in an awkward attempt at a bow. "Didn't mean to frighten you. See? I was wearing an invisibility cloak! Don't look so surprised. You're free!"

According to J. R. R. Tolkien, one of the major functions of fantasy is to provide readers with a means of escape. Some educators and literary critics might hasten to agree—with a sneer. But Tolkien wasn't sneering when he said it.

> Why should a man be scorned if, finding himself in
> prison, he tries to get out and go home? Or if, when he
> cannot do so, he thinks and talks about other topics than
> jailers and prison-walls?[27]

His point, of course, was that men and women really are prisoners. Fantasies, fairy tales, and dreams of escape are legitimate exercises for the human imagination, says Tolkien, because the human race does, in fact, stand in desperate need of rescue and release.

Our last reflection, "Impossible Odds," has already touched upon this idea. But there's a sense in which the intensely personal and individual struggle portrayed in Hans Christian Andersen's tale of Karen and the Red Shoes doesn't quite indicate the full scope of the problem. Karen's isn't just a private dilemma. Her deadly fascination with the Red Shoes isn't an isolated case. It's indicative of a pandemic disease—sin and the human predilection for self-willed rebellion against God. And the impossible grace she experienced at the moment of her release isn't merely the remedy for one quirky little girl's bizarre oddities and addictions. It's a cure for the ills of the entire race.

Like Karen, we all want healing. Like the enchanted young nobles in Galligantua's courtyard, we all desperately need to be transformed and liberated. But as a people—an enslaved and oppressed people like the children of Israel in Egypt—we require something more for our rescue and redemption than a moment of private enlightenment or a bit of personalized religion. An analyst or an adviser, a psychologist, counselor, pastor, or priest—none of these is big enough to fit the bill. What we want is a *Deliverer*.

Fairy tales recognize and celebrate this basic human need. The Redeemer, the Rescuer, the Conquering Hero is a familiar figure in the world of myth and fantasy. And Jack the Giant-Killer, the celebrated young gallant of the familiar English tale, is the quintessential image of the type.

Who is Jack? He's a farmer's only son from the Land's End of England, a poor and lowborn lad who is nevertheless "brisk and of a ready, lively wit."[28] Not a prince or a king, not a knight in shining armor, but a simple, resourceful peasant boy. That's why he's so uniquely and eminently qualified to be the Deliverer. Jack is one of us. And as one of us, he does what none of us could ever hope to do. Single-handedly he destroys the oppressor. He slips past obstacles and opposition, tears down fortresses, and sets the prisoners free. That's why Jack is our hero.

Jack is a great deal like that other unassuming rustic of biblical fame, David the shepherd, who also killed a giant and delivered his people from the despotism of a cruel and powerful enemy. In the imagination of the ancient Israelites, David quickly came to occupy the place of the ideal Deliverer, the archetypal Conqueror we all long to welcome with palm branches and triumphal processions. It's a position he has held among the Jews ever since. For to be the Son of David is to be the Hebrew *mashiach:* the Messiah, the Chosen One, the King anointed to save and set His people free.

The early Christians felt this yearning as intensely as their Jewish spiritual forefathers. "The Deliverer will come out of Zion," wrote the apostle Paul, harking back to the Psalms and the Prophets (Psalm 14:7; Isaiah 59:20), "and He will turn away ungodliness from Jacob" (Romans 11:26).

Jesus, of course, made no bones whatsoever about His claim to be that Deliverer. Even in His hometown, where it's always hard to live down the prejudices of relatives, neighbors, and friends, He didn't hesitate to walk into the synagogue, take up the scroll of Isaiah, and apply the following passage to Himself:

> The Spirit of the LORD is upon Me,
> Because He has anointed Me
> To preach the gospel to the poor;
> He has sent Me to heal the brokenhearted,
> To proclaim liberty to the captives
> And recovery of sight to the blind,
> To set at liberty those who are oppressed;
> To proclaim the acceptable year of the LORD.
>             (Luke 4:18-19)

If for a moment we can place ourselves inside the final episode of "Jack the Giant-Killer," we may begin to get some idea of what Jesus' claim really signifies. Picture yourself—a mole or a snake or a badger—inside that high-walled courtyard alongside the young duchess and her fellow captives. Imagine the hopelessness of your plight. Look up and cringe at the sight of the giant's red, grizzled, flabby-cheeked face. Hear the grating drone of his endless taunts. Feel the helpless terror of being reduced to the status of an animal—corralled, locked up without hope of release.

Now cock your ear and listen. Do you hear it? The sound of a trumpet! The unmistakable golden peal that alone spells the demise of the demagogue! The clarion call that proclaims "liberty throughout all the land to all its inhabitants" (Leviticus 25:10). Jack, by means of his invisible coat, his cap of knowledge, and his shoes of swiftness, has slipped past the watchful griffins. He has made his way to the gate. He has sounded the trumpet, and the walls of the prison are coming down!

The New Testament's picture of Christ's final victory over Death and Hell is every bit as colorful, as dramatic, and as earthshaking as the storyteller's account of Jack's triumph over Galligantua. Should we expect anything less where the liberation of the entire planet and the emancipation of the human race are at stake?

> The sun will be darkened, and the moon will not give its
> light; the stars will fall from heaven, and the powers of the
> heavens will be shaken. Then…they will see the Son of
> Man coming on the clouds of heaven with power and
> great glory. And He will send His angels with a great
> sound of a trumpet, and they will gather together His
> elect from the four winds, from one end of heaven to the
> other. (Matthew 24:29-31)

Glad tidings! Tidings of peace! Tidings of Jesus—of redemption and release! That's the clarion call of freedom, the great good news that each one of us is straining to hear.

# Royal Surprise

## *Reversing the Order*

### "Cinderella" from Charles Perrault and the Brothers Grimm

*The two sisters recognized her for the beautiful person*
*whom they had seen at the ball,*
*and threw themselves at her feet, begging her pardon*
*for all the ill-treatment she had suffered at their hands.*

Lentils in the ashes. It was a sort of game they played with her. A game for *them,* at any rate. She'd never seen much sport in it herself.

Tiny, flat, circular lentils. The smallest of beans. They'd dump a whole basket of them into the ashes on the hearth. Then they'd tell her to get busy and pick them out with her fingers, one by one, and have them all washed and cooked by supper. Then they'd laugh.

That's why she spent so much time squatting in the cinders, her hands and arms black to the elbows, her pretty face smudged beyond recognition. That's why her stepmother and older stepsister had gleefully christened her "Cinder-Slut." The younger stepsister wasn't half so vicious. She called her "Cinder-Ella."

Was she surprised when they kept her from attending the prince's ball? Not a bit. It was the *way* her stepmother had gone about it on this particular occasion, making a cruel and sarcastic joke of the whole affair, that had hurt so badly.

"Certainly you may go to the ball," she had said with a narrow-eyed, thin-lipped smile. "But first…"

First the lentils.

Fortunately, there were a great many things the spiteful woman hadn't taken into account. Things unseen and beyond the compass of narrow, grasping souls. Things like fairy godmothers and pumpkin coaches and lizard footmen. And the irrepressible power of the truth.

And so Cinderella *had* gone to the ball after all. Even now as she sat in the cinders, she was reliving the glories of that wondrous night, smiling to herself as she picked through the ashes. If they only knew! But of course they never would.

"Are you quite certain, Madame?"

A voice out in the hall! Her curiosity piqued, she dropped another lentil into the pot with a tiny, dull *clink,* ran to the door, and peeped out. There stood a man in the red uniform of a royal equerry. He was speaking to her stepmother and stepsisters.

"No other young ladies residing in the house?" he was saying. "None whatsoever? My orders are that *every* young maiden in the land must have an opportunity to try the glass slipper."

*Glass slipper!* The blood rushed to her face. She reached into the pocket of her apron and fingered the little clear glass shoe she had worn to the ball on that night of nights. The other had fallen off as she rushed down the palace steps at midnight.

"There is our servant girl," the younger stepsister was giggling.

"But she's dirty and deformed," added the elder in an irritated voice.

"Not even worth mentioning," said the stepmother coldly.

"No matter," said the officer with a sniff. "I must see her at once!"

Cinderella stepped into the light. He bade her sit down and put the slipper to her foot. It was a perfect fit.

"I have the other one," she said, glancing up and drawing the shoe's mate from her pocket. "If that makes any difference."

"Any difference!" exclaimed the equerry, an expression of joy mingled with relief passing over his lined and weary face. "My dear girl! It makes all the difference in the world! It means that you are to be the prince's wife!"

The stepmother turned livid. With a pale, flickering light in her deep-set eyes, she stumbled three steps backward and collapsed into an armchair.

But the two stepsisters looked at the ragged and sooty young girl with terror and recognition in their eyes.

"Forgive us!" they cried, falling down before her. "We didn't know it was you!"

⚜

"We didn't know it was you!" declare the two stepsisters, bowing at Cinderella's feet. And with that we come to the climactic moment of the story—the moment of utter and absolute *reversal*.

Reversal. Turnabout. The unexpected twist. It's the heart and soul of all good drama and storytelling. That's because it also happens to be the key to adventurous living—not to mention the fulcrum upon which the judgment and redemption of the world will one day turn.

"Cinderella" is perhaps the best known of all the "reversal stories" in the vast corpus of the world's fairy-tale literature. It's the tale of a young girl of high and noble birth, stripped of her rightful inheritance by usurpers, despised, rejected, subjugated, and treated like scum. She lives in her own house, among her own possessions, as a servant held in contempt. Smeared with soot, covered with the ashes of sorrow, she succumbs so completely to the marring effects of her circumstances that her true identity is obscured. She has no form or comeliness, no beauty that any should desire her.

But "Cinderella" is also the account of how this same disenfranchised maiden is suddenly lifted up out of this pit of miry clay. It's the story of an impossible intervention, a cataclysmic, eucatastrophic miracle that completely overturns her misery within the span of a single night. Yet this reversal does more than reverse. Cinderella is not merely restored to her rightful place as the daughter of a rich and prosperous merchant. Instead, she is elevated to the status of royalty—to the discomfiture of some and the great surprise of all concerned.

This is a common theme in the lore of Faerie. Time and time again it is the youngest, the smallest, the most despised brother who shocks the world by rising to the occasion and emerging victorious against impossible odds. It is the ugly duckling who proves to be a swan. The goose girl who turns out to be the king's true bride. The simpleton who marries a princess and becomes ruler of twelve kingdoms. Like Boots (or "Cinderlad"), hero of the Scandinavian tale "The Princess on the Glass Hill." Boots is a ten-time loser who, in the final moments of the story, is revealed to be a hero of almost superhuman stature:

"How, now," said the king; "have you got the golden apple? Speak out!"

"Yes, I have," said Boots; "here is the first, and here is the second, and here is the third too," and with that he pulled all three golden apples out of his pocket, and at the same time threw off his sooty rags, and stood before them in his gleaming golden mail.[29]

*Who would have thought it?* That's the question with which this kind of tale leaves its reader. Who would have guessed that the girl sitting in the cinders would one day be queen? That the empty-headed son of a poor widow could throw down a giant and go home with a fortune? That a harping, singing, stone-slinging shepherd boy would rise to the throne of Israel?

As with good drama, effective storytelling, and authentic living, so with the gospel; the elements of reversal and surprise lie at its very core. The history of humanity's redemption, and especially of the Redeemer who accomplished it, is, in fact, a "Cinderella story." The Son of God has come among us looking like anything but the stereotypical Messiah. We have not known Him as a conqueror on horseback, but as a drooling infant in swaddling clothes; not as a general, a senator, or an emperor in purple, but as a dusty, hard-handed carpenter from a backwater town, an itinerant poet and preacher in homespun. The King of kings has arrived in our midst disguised as a humble, suffering servant. He has been arrested, insulted, beaten, and executed as a common criminal. The devastating light of His glory has been concealed from all but the most perceptive eyes—hidden behind a cloak of ash and dirt, flesh and blood, weakness and death.

But the story does not end there. For the ultimate reversal is yet to come:

> And being found in appearance as a man, He humbled
> Himself and became obedient to the point of death, even
> the death of the cross. Therefore God also has highly
> exalted Him and given Him the name which is above
> every name, that at the name of Jesus every knee should
> bow, of those in heaven, and of those on earth, and of
> those under the earth, and that every tongue should con-
> fess that Jesus Christ is Lord, to the glory of God the
> Father. (Philippians 2:8-11)

Mary the mother of Jesus foresaw this dramatic twist and sang of it in the *Magnificat:*

> He has put down the mighty from their thrones,
> And exalted the lowly. (Luke 1:52)

Who would have thought it? Some, perhaps. But not many. And this is why, in the style of a true fairy-tale turnaround, that day of final reckoning will overtake the world like the coming of a thief in the night. When in the end the glass slipper is produced and He appears as undisputed Sovereign and Lord, some—those who have been looking forward to the event with eager anticipa- tion—will leap and dance for joy. But others are in for a royal sur- prise. Like the cruel stepsisters, they will suddenly find themselves face to face with the gravity of their error. In an instant, their attitude and position will shift from one of smug self-satisfaction to that of terror and desperate entreaty:

> And I will pour on the house of David and on the inhabitants of Jerusalem the Spirit of grace and supplication; then they will look on Me whom they pierced. Yes, they will mourn for Him as one mourns for his only son, and grieve for Him as one grieves for a firstborn. (Zechariah 12:10)

"We didn't know it was you!" That was the stepsisters' cry when the heart-stopping truth at last came to light. And in Perrault's version, their plea gains them a gracious pardon. But the Grimms, as usual, bring the tale to a far more sobering conclusion: "They were punished with blindness for the rest of their lives due to their wickedness and malice." [30]

Apparently it's worth ending up on the right side of this Great Divide.

> Sweet little Jesus boy,
> Lyin' in a manger;
> Sweet little Holy Child,
> We didn't know who you was. [31]

# Matchstick Kingdom

## Poverty's Paradox

"The Little Match-Girl" by Hans Christian Andersen

> *She wanted to keep herself warm, they said;*
> *but no one knew what beautiful things she had seen,*
> *nor in what radiance she had gone*
> *with her old granny into the joy of the New Year.*

Ringlets of gold at the nape of her neck, encrusted with gathering crystals of ice. Bare feet on snow-covered cobblestones, blue and red with the cold. Cheeks like winter roses. Bright eyes flashing behind a veil of swirling whiteness; eyes liquid and sparkling against the dull, flat backdrop of passing black hats and overcoats.

Such were the fleeting impressions the little girl left upon the mind of any passerby who happened to notice her. She was a small but painfully conspicuous speck at the heart of the city's endless drone and bustle.

The city held no place for her, had no need of her. That much seemed clear. Not a single match had she been able to sell all day long, though she carried bundles and bundles of them in her ragged old apron. Why should they buy her matches anyway? They all had lovely warm drawing rooms and humming stoves at home.

"Sell these matches in the city," her father had told her.

"Don't come home until you've sold them all! Bring the money to me, or I'll take it out of your hide!"

She shook her head. If only old Granny were home waiting for her. Granny had always been kind. Granny had been her one friend and protector. But Granny was dead...a whole year now. As things stood, she simply couldn't go home.

Dusk. The cold was deep and cruel and tenacious. Her fingers stung. Her toes she could not feel at all. Blowing on her hands and stamping, she pushed her way blindly through the crowd with no destination in mind.

Looking up, she a saw a narrow sheltered corner where one house jutted out a little beyond the next. Shivering, she huddled down in that out-of-the-way spot, took one of the matches in her trembling hand, and struck it against the wall.

Ah! The marvelous warmth of the match's tiny flame was like the breath of heaven upon the tips of her numbing fingers. She stretched out her toes, held the match above them, and smiled. Was any girl in the world happier than she? Had any other ever known such bliss?

As she watched, a vision emerged from within the circle of the flame's yellow glow: an iron stove with polished handles and fittings and a tongue of red fire dancing within its gaping mouth. And behind that, a room with lace curtains and a long table spread with white linen and set with silver and fine china. The table was heavy with a sumptuous New Year's Eve dinner: steaming roast goose, thick black pudding, prunes, apples, and nuts. The little girl drank in the aroma, she sucked it down greedily, she held her breath, and then—the match went out and the vision disappeared!

Quickly she struck another. Oh, glory! This time it was a Christmas tree decked with a thousand candles! And now the candles were rising, mounting into the velvet blue sky, turning into the stars of heaven itself. One of them fell in a long silvery streak just as the match sputtered out, and she remembered her old Granny's words: "When a star falls, a soul ascends to God."

Darkness again. Darkness and bleak cold. Once more she struck a match. Slowly a tall, graceful figure took shape within the glowing ring before her eyes. It was Granny herself! Granny transformed—beautiful as a shining angel!

"Oh, take me with you!" cried the little girl. "Don't leave me! Don't disappear like the stove and the roast goose and the bright Christmas tree!"

In desperation she realized the flame mustn't be allowed to go out! She would give everything to keep it alive, to hold the heavenly vision before her eyes! Without hesitating, she struck every last match in the bundle.

Up flared the bright yellow tongues against the gathering night, casting long and guttering black shadows up and over the silent stone walls of the houses. Granny smiled, reached down, and took the little girl by the hand. Then she lifted her up on her arm, and together they flew away through the falling snow, beyond the clouds, past the stars, and straight into the unspeakable joys of heaven, where cold, hunger, and fear were no more than a distant memory.

"Pitiful," said the constable as he sat at tea the following afternoon, telling his wife about it: a small body and a pile of burnt-out matches found in a dirty corner at the end of a dismal street. "Seems she was trying to keep herself warm."

He finished off a raspberry tart, put down his cup, and got up from the table. He hadn't a single thought for Christmas trees, falling stars, or transfigured grannies.

"What's for supper?" he said.

❧

Hans Andersen's "The Little Match-Girl" is a study in contrasts. Polarity and paradox meet us at every turn in this plain, almost plotless, but intensely powerful little story. It's filled with antithetical pairs. Beauty and harshness. Innocence and cruelty. Love and indifference. Childish simplicity and adult obtuseness. Poverty and wealth.

What does it all mean? Why, in the very throes of death, is this insignificant and impoverished little child granted such tantalizing visions of plenty and satiety and perfect joy? Why, at the mere flick of a match, is she given such dazzling glimpses of the kingdom beyond the veil? In the midst of her misery she receives a taste of heaven. Meanwhile, out in the street, people of wealth, sophistication, and intelligence rush by, too harried to notice, too busy to care. Afterward, they sit warming themselves in their parlors, numbing their senses with food and mulled wine while she freezes to death on a curbstone. The tale is a painful paradox in itself: inspirational and scandalous at once.

Jesus liked this kind of paradox. In fact, He was a master of the genre. His Beatitudes, which serve as a prologue to the famous

Sermon on the Mount, are perhaps the greatest example of His artistry and genius in the use of this strikingly effective rhetorical device:

> Blessed are the poor in spirit,
>> For theirs is the kingdom of heaven.
> Blessed are those who mourn,
>> For they shall be comforted.
> Blessed are the meek,
>> For they shall inherit the earth.
> Blessed are those who hunger and thirst for righteousness,
>> For they shall be filled. (Matthew 5:3-6)

Talk about a study in contrasts! How can the spiritually destitute inherit the spiritual kingdom? How can the sad be happy? Isn't that an oxymoron? How will the meek and self-effacing ever get ahead in the world? Doesn't nature itself teach us that only the strongest survive while nice guys finish last?

When it comes to God's kingdom, nothing is quite what we had expected. All of our preconceived notions must be set aside. Small is great. Wisdom is foolishness. Weakness turns out to be strength. Sorrow becomes joy. Death is the key to life. And, as in the story of "The Little Match-Girl," poverty is wealth. *Paradox,* Jesus seems to say, is essential to His message. The kingdom He proclaims is a kingdom of contrasts and contradictions.

That first beatitude, by the way, assumes an even starker form in Luke's gospel. In Luke, Jesus pushes the envelope a shocking inch or two further by suggesting that it's not only the *spiritually* poor who have a leg up on the kingdom, but the *economically* poor as well. Luke's is perhaps the bitterer pill to swallow, but it complements Andersen's story all the more tellingly:

> Blessed are you poor,
>> For yours is the kingdom of God. (Luke 6:20)

Luke underscores the point by giving us the other half of this particular contrasting couplet. Just four verses later Jesus turns around and says,

> But woe to you who are rich,
>> For you have received your consolation. (Luke 6:24)

Can this be right? Is Scripture really trying to tell us that God has a preference for derelicts? That He likes the poor better than the rich? Losers better than winners? Granted, that's a rather bald and artless way of stating it, yet from Genesis to Revelation a consistent thread of argumentation appears to make this very case. Quietly but persistently, over and over again, the biblical poets, prophets, and apostles insist that the poor of this world really are in some sense the recipients of God's special care and concern:

> He will spare the poor and needy,
> And will save the souls of the needy.
> He will redeem their life from oppression and violence;
> And precious shall be their blood in His sight.
>> (Psalm 72:13-14)

Has God not chosen the poor of this world to be rich in
faith and heirs of the kingdom which He has promised to
those who love Him? (James 2:5)

This is the message that comes through loud and clear in the
story of "The Little Match-Girl." It's not a message about the
need for social reform or the importance of feeding the hungry.
Nor is it a call to give generously or get involved in assistance pro-
grams—though we can and should do all these things wherever
and whenever we have opportunity (Deuteronomy 15:11; John
12:8). The tale of "The Little Match-Girl" is about something far
simpler and more profound. It tells us that when we are among
the poor, we are in some sense in the presence of our betters—
our superiors and senior partners in the life of the kingdom and
the things of the Spirit. As James says,

Let the lowly brother glory in his exaltation, but the rich
in his humiliation. (James 1:9-10)

In earthly terms, the Little Match-Girl is as poor as poor can
be. And yet out of the very matchsticks of her poverty arise rich
visions of the unseen realm and the life to come, visions granted
only to a select few. Why is she chosen to receive them? Because
she is in such desperate need. She yearns for her Granny and for
God in heaven because, unlike the comfortable townsfolk around
her, she has nothing else. And it's precisely in this sense that her
poverty is wealth: It drives her, as nothing else can, to seek the
things above (Colossians 3:1).

This, it seems, is why the poor qualify for a special measure of God's favor. They realize their abject need. They know beyond a shadow of a doubt that they are not, never have been, and never will be self-sufficient. Therefore, God has placed the wealth of the universe at their fingertips. It's theirs for the asking. And they will experience it in all its fullness when at last He calls them home to Himself.

Is it any wonder Jesus came preaching a gospel of paradox? He brought His good news to the poor (Luke 4:18) precisely because the poor have ears to hear it. They already know what the rest of us spend a lifetime trying to learn: Our cups must be empty to receive the fullness of God's blessings.

# FLiGHT

*Soaring on Wings of Childlike Faith*

"Peter Pan" by J. M. Barrie

*They were all on their beds, and gallant Michael let go first.*
*He did not quite mean to let go, but he did it,*
*and immediately he was borne across the room.*
*"I flewed!" he screamed while still in mid-air.*

Wendy was spellbound. *What would it be like?* she wondered as Peter took another turn past the mantelpiece and made a second circuit of the room, his hair just brushing the ceiling. On the third pass he glanced down at her—as if to make sure of his audience—and crowed. A fiercely defiant and joyous crow. Wendy sighed.

To fly! Just think of it! Free of every hindrance and encumbrance! Soaring, banking, swooping! Out the window, over the river, beyond the sea, and back again. She pictured herself high in the moonlight, circling the house, diving straight into the nursery, landing in a graceful arabesque upon the dresser. *Heavenly* was the word that came to mind.

Peter, chin up and arms folded across his chest, floated to a sitting position atop the bedpost.

"How do you do it?" asked John breathlessly. Then, too eager to wait for an answer, he leaped off the bed and fell heavily against the foot of the wardrobe. Michael followed suit, with similar results.

Peter hugged his knees and laughed aloud. Wendy glanced at him and pouted.

"But you make it look so delightfully easy!" she protested.

"It *is* easy," he said, cocking his head and arching an eyebrow. "You just think lovely, wonderful thoughts." As if to demonstrate, he closed his eyes and rose slowly toward the ceiling. "See?"

She tried it. Mermaids. Lagoons. Moonlight on glossy green tropical leaves. A snug little house, herself in an apron, Peter with slippers and pipe. Her stomach fluttered. She squeezed her eyes tight, trying hard to believe it. But it was no use.

"Perhaps you'd better teach us," said John, rising stiffly from yet another crash landing. He readjusted his glasses and smoothed the front of his nightshirt in an attempt to restore his injured dignity.

But Peter only laughed again. "I was just playing with you!" he said. "Didn't you know? Faith and trust—that's all it takes— *and* a pinch of fairy dust!"

With that he cupped a hand to his mouth and blew upon the children. A delicate cloud of glittering green and gold rose into the air and settled over their hair and faces and shoulders. Wendy twitched. John sneezed.

"Now *let go!*" Peter shouted—for they were all sitting on the edges of their beds, clutching the rumpled bedclothes in their fists. Michael did let go, and off he soared, squealing like a delighted little pig. An unanticipated flash of joy pierced Wendy's heart like a lightning bolt. Without thinking, she released her hold on the coverlet. In a moment, all three of them were dashing after Peter in a mad, merry chase around the upper reaches of the nursery, laughing and shouting.

All at once the window blew open, and the sounds of Mr. and Mrs. Darling's returning footsteps reached them from below.

"Quick!" Peter cried in his captain voice. "Out the window!" In the next instant, Wendy's vision had all come true: the Thames below them, the clouds above, the moonlit rooftops of the houses wheeling away behind. Again she sighed—a slow, delicious sigh...

"What is it, Mother?"

Wendy started at the sound of her daughter's voice. She shook herself and opened her eyes.

"I was just remembering, Jane. That's all," she said.

"Remembering?"

"Yes. Remembering what it was like...to fly."

A pair of wide blue eyes stared up at her. "But can't you fly now?"

The mother smiled sadly. "No, my sweet. I'm grown up now, you see. And when people grow up—well, they forget the way. They forget how to be trusting and careless. They forget how to *let go.*" She turned and looked down at the little girl. "I don't suppose you understand what I mean..."

But Jane wasn't listening. She was on her feet, her eyes fixed on the nursery window. "Do you hear it, Mother?" she asked. "Do you hear it?"

And Wendy, who had to admit that she did, involuntarily shrunk into herself and pretended that she didn't.

But Jane went bounding across the room and threw open the window.

Outside, someone was crowing.

❖

"I don't want ever to be a man! I want always to be a little boy and to have fun!"

That's what he says the very first time we meet him—the inimitable Peter Pan. In these few words he sums up the spirit of both the man and the age that gave him birth: writer J. M. Barrie and the Victorian-Edwardian era.

William Wordsworth, writing in the early part of the nineteenth century, foreshadowed that spirit in his famous ode "Intimations of Immortality." The poem celebrates the wonder and glory of childhood…and laments its gradual and inevitable fading away:

> Trailing clouds of glory do we come
> > From God, who is our home:
> Heaven lies about us in our infancy![32]

A magical flight, "trailing clouds of glory." The experience which of all earthly experiences brings us closest to heaven. This was Wordsworth's vision of childhood. This was his measure of its significance.

He was not alone in this sentiment. For nearly half a century—from the 1860s to the beginning of the Great War in 1914—English art and culture revolved around what some have called an "obsession" with this ideal. Not surprisingly, it was during this period that most of our classic children's fantasies were written, books like *Alice's Adventures in Wonderland, The Wind in the Willows, Puck of Pook's Hill, The Enchanted Castle, The Secret Garden,* the stories of Beatrix Potter, the "nonsense" lyrics of Edward Lear…and, of course, Barrie's *Peter Pan.*

In our own time, historians and critics have given the Victorian fascination with children and childhood a rather pathological interpretation. They understand it as a reaction against restrictive social mores. "In fantasy," writes author Jackie Wullschläger, "unconscious or repressed desires could be expressed, and this is why strict and sombre Victorian England inspired so great an outburst of anarchic, escapist, nonsensical children's books."[33]

Meanwhile, modern psychologists and cultural commentators have often made Peter Pan into a symbol of one of the most notorious social scourges of our own era: the irresponsible adult male. It has been said, and rightly so, that a majority of our present-day cultural ills—family breakdown, teen pregnancy, drug abuse, abortion, divorce, and a score of related plagues—can be traced to the attitudes and actions of men who "want always to be little boys and to have fun."

What are we to make of all this? Is Peter nothing but the figment of a frustrated, repressed, and psychologically twisted mind? Can anything good come of the wild and reckless boy who once told Mrs. Darling, "Keep back, lady, no one is going to catch me and make me a man!"

It can, and for a reason we dare not miss. For as it turns out, Wordsworth was right. There is something marvelous and venerable, something almost *sacred* about childhood. Children do

come to us fresh from the hand of God, "trailing clouds of glory."
Children are precious and inexpressibly valuable in His sight. Any
society that exploits, abuses, and destroys its own children is a
society near to the brink of hell itself. How do we know this? The
Bible tells us so.

Where, after all, did Barrie and the Victorians get this idea of
a child who would prefer to remain a child? It would have been
unthinkable in the pre-Christian world. In that world, childhood
was a precarious, endangered, and highly unenviable state. The
merchants of Tyre and Sidon sacrificed children to the god Baal.
Educated Greeks and fashionable Romans left unwanted babies
to die of exposure on barren hillsides. Down through the ages, in
the great civilizations as well as in primitive tribal settings, children have been valued mainly for their potential as future adults
—not for what they are in and of themselves.

But all this changes when God appears on earth in the form
of a slumbering babe. Here indeed is a thing fearfully marvelous
and new: an exaltation of children and childhood apart from
which the story of Peter and Wendy would have been inconceiv-
able. This is why G. K. Chesterton insisted that "Peter Pan does
not belong to the world of Pan but the world of Peter":[34]

And she brought forth her firstborn Son, and
wrapped Him in swaddling cloths, and laid Him in
a manger....
    And the Child grew and became strong in spirit,
filled with wisdom; and the grace of God was upon Him.
(Luke 2:7,40)

Once He had grown to manhood, that Child took this same idea and pushed it even further. In words that must have shaken some of His self-satisfied contemporaries to the soles of their sandals, Jesus proclaimed that children are not merely valuable in and of themselves. On the contrary, children also have a great deal to teach us. As a matter of fact, when it comes to the things of God, children have a distinct advantage over their grown-up counterparts:

> At that time the disciples came to Jesus, saying, "Who then is greatest in the kingdom of heaven?"
>
> Then Jesus called a little child to Him, set him in the midst of them, and said, "Assuredly, I say to you, unless you are converted and become as little children, you will by no means enter the kingdom of heaven. Therefore whoever humbles himself as this little child is the greatest in the kingdom of heaven." (Matthew 18:1-4)

> Let the little children come to Me, and do not forbid them; for of such is the kingdom of God. Assuredly, I say to you, whoever does not receive the kingdom of God as a little child will by no means enter it. (Mark 10:14-15)

"Of such is the kingdom of God." This is a radical, earth-shaking phrase. Is it possible that children are in some sense inherently higher, holier, and closer to the heart of God than adult men and women? Yes, says Jesus. Because children, He implies, know how to fly. They have an inherent talent for mounting up "with wings like eagles" (Isaiah 40:31). They are near to the kingdom—indeed, they are entering into it ahead of many who are much older and wiser—not because they are pure and free from sin (we know very well that they're not), but because they know how to trust. They understand intuitively and instinctively what it means to soar on the wings of faith. They are not above letting go and allowing someone else to carry them. They have yet to unlearn the habits and attitudes we adults have spent so many decades acquiring and honing to perfection: worry, anxiety, self-determination, and stubborn pride.

Why do grownups forget how to fly? According to Barrie, it's because they are no longer "gay and innocent and heartless."[35] By "heartless," he did not mean "cruel" or "lacking in compassion." The sense he must certainly have intended is "wild, abandoned, free from care."

The message is unmistakable. With Peter Pan, the eternal child, we can rise above the rooftops and the clouds. We can leave the wearing and wearying trials of day-to-day life far behind. We can do it if, like gallant Michael, we will simply *let go*—let go and allow ourselves to soar.

How is this possible? The answer is simple. Be converted. Become like little children. "Cast all your anxiety on him because he cares for you" (1 Peter 5:7, NIV).

It's as easy—and as difficult—as flying.

# Ragtag Band

## The Refugee Church

"The Bremen Town Musicians" from the Brothers Grimm

*Why don't you come along with us?…*
*We're off to Bremen*
*where there are better things than death.*

Poor old donkey. He was good for nothing.

That's what the master and mistress said anyway. Too old to work. Too weak to bear burdens. Too expensive to feed. He knew how they talked: "Dog meat. Pennies per pound."

So when the night was dark and the moon had slipped behind a cloud, he made for the road and set out for Bremen, where he intended to become a musician. Who could blame him?

The dog's situation wasn't much better. He was in a sorry state when old Long Ears found him by the roadside, panting and heaving as if he'd never catch his breath.

*"Wauwau! Ich bin Flüchtling!"* he said in answer to the donkey's questioning looks. "Master says I've outlived my usefulness. I'm running away!"

"You don't say?" said the donkey. "My situation exactly! Why don't you come with me to Bremen? We'll be town musicians! It's better than the glue factory!"

The dog couldn't argue with that.

The cat was sitting on a fence post wearing a long, sad face when the two traveling troubadours came by.

"*Wehe mir!*" she moaned. "Woe is me! I'm finished as a mouser! My teeth are worn and dull! Mistress wants to drown me! *Mir, mir, wehe mir!*"

"I've heard your nighttime serenades," said the dog, wincing slightly. "If you'd like"—he paused and gave the donkey a side-wise glance—"well, you might come along with us to Bremen. We're going to be musicians!"

The donkey nodded enthusiastically. The cat soon agreed. It was by far the best offer she'd had.

The three companions hadn't traveled more than a mile or so when they passed a farm. High above the gate perched a rooster, crowing his very heart out.

"*Ach! Ach! Unglücklicher Ich!*" he screamed. "Tomorrow's Sunday and guests are coming for dinner! My head comes off tonight!"

"It would be silly to wait around for that!" said the donkey. "Why don't you come with us? We're going to Bremen where there are better things than death!"

The rooster was quick to see the advantages of the donkey's plan. After all, he took pride in his fine tenor voice. And he was rather inclined to hold on to his head for as long as possible.

Off they went, then, the four of them raising a loud and rau-cous chorus all along the road. But the journey was long, and Bremen was still far off when dusk overtook them. Hungry, thirsty, and bone-tired, they were seeking a suitable spot for the night in a forested glade when the rooster, who had taken up his watch post at the top of a tree, began to sing out.

"*Kikeriki!*" he crowed. "A light! A light! I see a light in the wood!"

It was a robber's den! They approached cautiously.

"There's a table inside," whispered the donkey, peering in through the dingy little window, "just loaded with food! And a fire on the hearth!"

"What good is it to us?" hissed the cat.

"Yes—with armed desperadoes on every side," observed the rooster.

"And we being old and weak and useless," muttered the dog.

The donkey eyed them sagely. "By ourselves," he said, "not one of us could manage it. But together—ah, together we may! Are we not musicians?"

With that, he assumed the role of *Konzertmeister*, kicked up his heels, and set up a loud braying. The others joined in, barking, yowling, and cock-a-doodle-doing with all their might. Then up jumped the donkey and shattered the window with his two front hoofs. Out of the house dashed the robbers in a terrible fright, screaming, "Monsters! Demons! Devils!" In marched the four troubadours.

It's said that the neighborhood was rid of a band of ruthless cutthroats that day.

As for the musicians, they eventually made it to Bremen as planned. But they liked the little house in the woods so much that they found themselves returning to it often.

As often as their touring schedule would permit.

❧

The few. The proud. Do you have what it takes to be one of them?

That's what you'll have to ask yourself if you're thinking about joining the U.S. Marines. It's no idle question. With a relentlessly discriminating eye, the corps solicits recruits of only the highest caliber—an elite cadre of handpicked cream-of-the-croppers. After that, by means of a rigorous regimen of blood, sweat, and tears, it proceeds to make them even fewer, prouder, and stronger than they were to begin with. The result? A lean, mean fighting machine, molded precisely to the manufacturer's specifications and design.

How different are the communities in which most of us live out our daily lives! We don't have the option of selecting our neighbors and coworkers. Unlike marine recruiters, we aren't granted the privilege of picking our companions and compatriots according to some predetermined standard of excellence. Unlike talent scouts and Hollywood film directors, we don't get to audition our brothers, sisters, and children, our aunts, uncles, and mothers-in-law before assigning them a part in the family cast. Even our spouses and best friends tend to "happen" to us as a result of circumstances beyond our control. When it comes to fellow travelers on the journey of life, we don't get what we choose. We get what we get.

So goes the Grimm brothers' tale of "The Bremen Town Musicians," the unlikeliest bunch of minstrels ever to land a gig at the local hofbrau. It wasn't by design that the old donkey, dog, cat, and rooster found themselves headed down the road toward their first-ever big-city engagement. The whole thing just sort of "fell together." They hadn't considered a musical career until the emergence of certain situations forced them to reevaluate their options. They didn't even know one another until necessity compelled them to cast their lot together in a common cause: to escape the edge of the ax.

So it was that they became traveling companions. They weren't in the least idealistic about their little band. "Few"—they were certainly that! But they had no illusions about being either "proud" or "strong." On the contrary, they were keenly conscious of having been driven to this mad course of action by their own weakness, feebleness, and apparent uselessness in the eyes of the world. Like Christian fleeing the City of Destruction in John Bunyan's *The Pilgrim's Progress,* they were running for their lives—not something to be particularly proud of.

If this principle of pragmatically determined random association is typical of most human partnerships, it's fair to say that it's eminently characteristic of the church, that haphazard band of pilgrims who call themselves followers of Jesus. We Christians don't have the luxury of selecting our brothers and sisters in the faith. The Master chooses them for us. That might not be so bad, except that His selection rarely coincides with our personal preferences. Much as we in our earthly wisdom might expect the Lord of Hosts to recruit His troops and muster His armies according to the foolproof methods of "the few, the proud, and the strong," He appears to operate on the basis of a rather different set of standards and assumptions. Bizarre, frustrating, and mystifying standards. Assumptions that seem to fly in the face of common sense.

Just take a look around next time you're in a gathering of Christians and see if this isn't so. The church, in its truest and most authentic form, is anything but an elite corps of highly qual- ified, top-flight special forces. Many of its members are not the kind of people with whom we'd elect to spend time if given the choice. If we're honest, we'll have to admit that there are actually large numbers of our fellow believers with whom we don't seem to have a great deal in common, people we find it hard to like, let alone love. That's because the church is not a political party, a social clique, or a special-interest club. Like the Bremen Town Musicians, it's something more in the nature of a scruffy, bedraggled col- lection of refugees and reluctant road warriors.

"You did not choose Me," says Jesus to His disciples, "but I chose you and appointed you that you should go and bear fruit" (John 15:16). And just whom does He choose? Fishermen. A shifty tax collector and Roman collaborator. An alienated politi- cal dissident. An arrogant Pharisee. A tentmaker, a tanner, and a prostitute.

Later Paul discerned a similar demographic profile among the membership of the church in Corinth:

> For you see your calling, brethren, that not many wise
> according to the flesh, not many mighty, not many
> noble, are called. But God has chosen the foolish things
> of the world to put to shame the wise, and God has
> chosen the weak things of the world to put to shame the
> things which are mighty; and the base things of the world
> and the things which are despised God has chosen, and
> the things which are not, to bring to nothing the things

that are, that no flesh should glory in His presence.
(1 Corinthians 1:26-29)

What was it that brought such a motley crew together? The answer is simple: Like the Bremen Town Musicians, they were fleeing for their lives. They had found the Messiah (John 1:41), and in Him they had discovered their last and only hope. Accordingly, they threw everything aside to follow Him down the road to a place where "there are things better than death." The result? An unplanned, unforeseen, ad hoc fellowship of outlandish miscellany and diversity. A fellowship of the faithful, fleeing few.

Author Vernard Eller explains it this way: Ever since the emperor Constantine legitimized and institutionalized the Christian movement, it has become customary to view the church as a kind of commissary—"an *institution* which has been *commissioned* to *dispense* particular goods, services, or benefits to a *select constituency.*" But the church, contends Eller, was never meant to be a commissary at all. "The New Testament," he claims, "pictures the church as a *caravan.*"

> A *caravan...* (and a *walking* caravan best fits our idea) is a group of people banded together to make *common cause* in seeking a *common destination.*[36]

This describes the Bremen Town Musicians perfectly. "We're off to Bremen where there are better things than death," they said. In this sense, the poor old donkey, dog, cat, and rooster call to mind those heroes and heroines of faith of whom the writer to the Hebrews says,

[They] confessed that they were strangers and pilgrims on the earth. For those who say such things declare plainly that they seek a homeland. And truly if they had called to mind that country from which they had come out, they would have had opportunity to return. But now they desire a better, that is, a heavenly country. Therefore God is not ashamed to be called their God, for He has prepared a city for them. (Hebrews 11:13-16)

As followers of the Lord Jesus, the Traveler who had "nowhere to lay His head" (Luke 9:58), we, too, are "strangers and pilgrims on the earth." Like the Bremen Town Musicians, we're a group of refugees, traveling down the road in search of that promised country, a place where there are "better things than death." We're a heaven-bound ragtag band—nothing more, nothing less.

# Stinging Nettles

## The Anguish of Redemption

"The Wild Swans" by Hans Christian Andersen

*"Oh, what is the pain in my fingers*
*to the agony my heart suffers!" she thought.*
*"I must risk it!"*

Elise stared in open-mouthed wonder as she glided down
through the dusky air. Quickly—for the sun was nearly
gone—the eleven swans dived and plummeted, swinging the
giddy girl earthward in her hammock of plaited rushes and wil-
low bark. They touched the ground just as the last golden spark
slipped away beneath the western horizon. Elise tumbled into the
sweet grass, tore up some of it in her fists, and kissed it.

She was sitting on a flowery blue hillside in front of a deep
cave. Cool and fragrant airs breathed softly from its wide mouth.
Delicate green creepers covered the ground in front of it like a
rich embroidered carpet. The flutter of the swans' white wings
and the harsh notes of their cries filled the air around her. Then
the last warm hint of the sun's rays faded from the sky, and in an
instant they were swans no more but handsome young men—
Elise's eleven enchanted brothers. Swans by day and men by
night.

After two full days of flying and a night on a rock in the

middle of the open sea, she was glad when they invited her to rest within the shadowed recesses of the cavern.

"If only I might dream of a way to set you all free!" she murmured, drifting off. So filled was her mind with this thought that she continued praying to God as she fell asleep, asking Him to show her how the enchantment might be broken...

Clouds again—plumes and columns and pillars of billowing white. She knew what it was: a fairy palace somewhere near the top of the sky. And now a voice reached her ears—low and indistinct at first, then clear and strong. She opened her eyes and found herself looking up into the face of a radiant fairy princess.

"Your brothers can be freed," said the fairy, a deep furrow creasing her brow, "but only at great cost! Can you endure the pain your delicate fingers must feel? Can you bear the anxiety and torment your heart must suffer?"

Elise looked up into the fairy's eyes. "I can!" she whispered. "I must!"

"And so you shall!" said the fairy. "Do you see this stinging nettle I am holding in my hand? Many of them grow around the cave where you are sleeping. Go out and pick them. Though they burn like fire and raise blisters on your skin, tread them with your bare feet. Twist the fibers into yarn with your bare hands. From this yarn knit eleven long-sleeved shirts. When you are finished, throw the shirts over the eleven wild swans and they will become men again—permanently! It is the only way to break the spell. But remember this: Until this task is finished—and it may take years—you must not speak! The first word you utter will pierce your brothers' hearts like a knife!"

Elise woke. Outside the cave feathery green nettles waved in the morning breeze. She jumped to her feet and ran out into the open air...

Gaunt and worn, she looked out over the sea of mocking faces that lined the street, as if the passage of time had stretched her thin. Furiously she knitted, her fingers flying, her mind teeming with thoughts of her brothers. It was the last sleeve of the last shirt! At the end of the thoroughfare she could see the scaffold and the stake piled high with firewood. From the curb the crowd hurled taunts at her: "Look at the witch with her beastly witchcraft! Take it away from her! Tear it into a thousand pieces!"

Even her royal husband, the king who had found her in the forest near the beginning of her ordeal, had not been able to save her. Accused of witchcraft, imprisoned, condemned, she was unable to speak a word in her own defense. Now she rode, bouncing and jogging, in a tumbrel over the cobbled lanes, knitting, knitting, knitting—pain and anguish behind her, certain death before her.

Suddenly there came a stirring of the air above her. Out of the sky, a storm of wings—glossy-white, rosy-tinted—swishing over her head and past her ear. In the next instant the swans settled to the ground in front of the cart just as it came to a stop before the platform. The executioner reached out to seize her. With one last desperate burst of energy, she struggled to her feet and cast the eleven shirts over the eleven great birds.

"Now I can speak!" Elise shouted. "I am innocent!"

"Yes!" agreed the eldest brother, who suddenly stood there at the head of a troop of eleven young princes, his dark hair glinting in the sunlight. "She is innocent!"

The pile of firewood burst into a hedge of a million fragrant red roses.

⚜

Wounded, bleeding hands and feet. Eyes dimmed by the sheer relentlessness of the pain, yet fixed unwaveringly upon the goal. A mission to be accomplished, a mind spinning with the realization of the high stakes, a heart fueled by the fires of love. Is this the stuff of children's nursery tales? Or is it rather the echo of a historic and heavenly struggle to redeem the human soul—the stuff of the gospel itself?

The stirring story of "The Wild Swans" begins like so many other good fairy tales—with a wicked stepmother. Elise's father, the king, has married a cruel woman who will go to any length to get rid of her stepchildren: a beautiful daughter and eleven stalwart sons. Elise, abused and tormented, is banished from the palace. Then the queen casts an evil spell over the boys:

> "Fly out into the world and shift for yourselves! Fly away
> like great birds without voices!" She had not the power,
> however, to do them all the evil she would, and they
> became eleven beautiful wild swans.[37]

How to redeem her brothers from this curse? That is the question that possesses the princess from this point forward. Ultimately her quest leads to a joyful end but not before traversing many thorny ways. For Elise soon learns that there is only one remedy for her brothers' plight: She must be willing to endure the pain of stinging nettles.

Stinging nettles. Have you ever taken a fool's shortcut through the woods and fallen into a patch of them? If so, you will have some idea of what it might be like to pluck them up by handfuls—deliberately. Without much effort you'll be able to feel their tiny pricking needlelike spines against your skin. Now push fancy a bit further and picture yourself trampling them, barefoot, into a workable pulp, then stretching the fibers into fine finger-rasping threads. Imagine the burning itch, the swelling redness, the rising welts on your hands, feet, and ankles.

Stinging nettles. The anguish of redeeming love. To think that one, the purest, tenderest, and most blameless of all, should bear this terrible agony for the rest. Those stinging nettles are the nucleus around which the tale of "The Wild Swans" revolves. At the story's dramatic climax, when the eleven brothers are restored at last, we know beyond a shadow of a doubt that they owe their release not merely to Elise's goodness, faithfulness, and loyalty, but preeminently to her willingness to endure the stinging nettles—her capacity for redemptive suffering.

Can we fail to think of Jesus, the trampled Rose of Sharon, the bruised Lily of the Valley, as we stand by and watch Elise, mocked by the crowds, riding to her death in an open cart? Like the fairy-tale princess, Christ did not shrink from the stinging nettles. He, too, bore the lash and wore the crown of thorns, enduring the cross and despising the shame "for the joy that was set before Him" (Hebrews 12:2). Just as Elise suffered for her brothers, He suffered on our behalf, and "by his wounds we are healed" (Isaiah 53:5, NIV).

> I gave My back to those who struck Me,
> And My cheeks to those who plucked out the beard;
> I did not hide My face from shame and spitting.
>         (Isaiah 50:6)

The blood of Jesus, the "Lamb who was slain," occupies a central place in orthodox Christian theology. Believers sing hymns about a "fountain filled with blood" and declare, "Nothing can for sin atone, nothing but the blood of Jesus." Isn't it amazing, then, how little time we spend thinking about the practical implications of these boldly worded phrases? All too often when we wear the cross on a silver chain around our necks or affix it to the top of church steeples, we forget that it was an instrument of torture and execution, a symbol of agony and death.

Deliverance from the bondage of sin and the enchantment of the devil does not come cheap. Just as the princess Elise had to endure pain, toil, misunderstanding, rejection, and condemnation in her quest to save her brothers, so Christ suffered all in order to redeem us from "the wages of sin," which is death (Romans 6:23). By no other means could the spell be broken.

But there's another nuance to this theme of the stinging nettles that we may find even more disturbing. For Elise's painful journey is not simply a beautiful and powerful parable of the anguish

Jesus endured on our behalf. It's also a picture of the pilgrimage to which *we* are called as His disciples.

"Remember the word that I said to you," Christ once reminded His followers. " 'A servant is not greater than his master.' If they persecuted Me, they will also persecute you" (John 15:20). This is a concept that first-century believers, in dramatic contrast to their modern spiritual heirs, seemed to take for granted. They understood implicitly that there is no higher calling than to become "partakers of [His] sufferings" (2 Corinthians 1:7) and to be "conformed to His death" (Philippians 3:10):

> For to you it has been granted on behalf of Christ, not
> only to believe in Him, but also to suffer for His sake.
> (Philippians 1:29)

What does it mean to identify with Christ's passion in this way? To become partakers of His sufferings, "conformed to His death"? These images conceal a mystery that we may never understand completely this side of eternity. And yet the Bible indicates that in some unexplained way, this aspect of the believer's experience in the world may bear a direct connection with the redemptive work of the Savior. In suffering with Christ, we, like Elise, may have some role to play in breaking the spell that holds our brothers and sisters captive:

> I now rejoice in my sufferings for you, and fill up in my
> flesh what is lacking in the afflictions of Christ, for the
> sake of His body, which is the church. (Colossians 1:24)

Stinging nettles. The anguish of redeeming love. It's not one of the gospel's stronger selling points—at least not in the marketplace of contemporary spiritual and religious ideas. But it *is* one of the greatest privileges we have been granted as joint heirs of the suffering Son of God.

The question is, Will we enter into it as willingly as Elise?

# Foam on the Water

## *Self-Emptying Love*

### "The Little Mermaid" by Hans Christian Andersen

*Hurry! Either he or you must die
before the sun rises!*

I t has all come to nothing.

Far off on the horizon, a ruddy glow was pushing up from beyond the rim of the world, tinting the tips of the restless waves with the dull glint of mottled bronze. She stood on the deck of the ship, a simple girl in a plain white linen shift, staring without emotion at her two bare feet.

Everything. She had traded *everything* for those two human feet. Not just her glistening fishtail, but her home, her family, her life below the sea, even her enchantingly beautiful voice. She had thrown it all away on a chance—a chance that hung by a doubtful thread.

And now the thread had snapped.

Voices came back to her as she leaned heavily against the rail and peered out over the ocean. Her grandmother's: "We mermaids can live three hundred years, but when our life is finished here, we are only foam upon the water." Her own: "I would risk everything to win him and an immortal soul!" The sea-witch's:

"The very first morning after he weds another, your heart will break, and you will become foam upon the water!"

The streak of light on the horizon grew brighter. The breeze stirred the tent flaps of the purple pavilion where the prince and his new bride lay sleeping. *The very first morning... All for nothing.* She had wagered all—and lost.

Looking out over the water, she noticed a disturbance just below the ship's prow. Bubbles, rings, a splash. Five shapely heads bobbed up above the waves. Five heads shorn of their lovely long golden hair. Her five sisters!

"Here!" shouted the eldest, reaching back and flinging something up at the deck. A bright object flashed in the air. She caught it by the handle. It was a long, sharp knife.

"We traded our hair to the sea-witch for it!" her sister was shouting. "Take it! Plunge it into his heart. It's your only hope. When his blood spurts onto your feet, they will grow together into a fishtail, and then you can come down to us again. Act quickly"—glancing over her shoulder at the pale eastern sky— "before the sun rises!"

She looked at the weapon in her hand. At this very moment he lay within the pavilion, another at his side. Another had won his heart. Another would walk beside him and share his life. Though she had given her all, he had chosen another. Perhaps her sisters were right...

They were calling to her from the water. "Hurry! *It's his life or yours!*"

*Foam on the water.* In a moment, in a matter of seconds, the first bright ray of the sun would come bursting over the edge of the ocean. She gripped the handle of the knife, stepped quickly to the pavilion, drew back the curtain, and stood over the sleeping pair.

She caught her breath at the sight of his face. It was so lovely, flushed with the ruddy light that poured in under the tent hangings. He lay in a dream. She saw him stir and turn in his sleep. She heard him murmur his bride's name. With trembling lip and shaking hand, she raised the knife.

And then she hesitated. Again her glance dropped to her feet. How she had longed to walk along the shore with him on long summer evenings, to step proudly at his side down city streets, to run barefoot with him through the flowering grass. Should she let those feet be spattered with his blood?

Abruptly she turned. Terrible as a storm she burst from the pavilion, flinging herself across the deck and up against the rail. With one great sweep of her arm, the knife flew glittering out over the water and disappeared beneath the waves. In the next moment the sun, blazing like burnished gold, jumped up above the horizon and caught her there, leaning out over the sea with outstretched arms. She jumped—and the very last thing she saw was the splash of her sisters' five fishtails as they flipped, dived, and fled into the depths of the ocean.

Slowly the sun rode higher. Gradually the sky turned blue. In its growing light the foam sparkled on the water.

Sea foam, golden in the sunrise…slowly dissolving on the surface of the sea.

⚜

Picture yourself at a sumptuous banquet. On the table before you a silver goblet brims with ruby red wine. Raise the cup to your lips. For the briefest moment, savor the wine's heady fragrance as it invades your nostrils. Imagine the pungent aroma caressing your taste buds.

Stop! Just before the sweet liquid touches your tongue, with a quick twist of your wrist, dump the precious fluid on the floor. All of it. Now shake the cup. Shake it again—harder this time. Be certain that not a single red droplet remains trembling on the edge of the vessel's smooth silver lip.

This word picture embodies an important biblical concept, represented by the Greek word *kenosis.* Theologians have invested this word with a unique and specific spiritual significance, particularly in the way they apply it to the person and life of Christ. It refers to a voluntary "emptying" or "pouring out," and it's related to a verb that classical authors used in the sense of "to drain" or "spill." In the New Testament it takes on an extended metaphorical meaning: "to make of no account or no effect."

The idea of *kenosis* has its roots in the ancient pagan custom of the *libation.* A libation was a kind of sacrifice—a ritual in which precious wine or oil was poured out upon the ground or over an altar in honor of a god or some human beneficiary. The imagery is striking. As the old saying goes, "There's no use crying over spilt milk."

Divested of its invisible religious significance, a libation poured out is nothing but pure waste. While it remains in the cup or cask, wine retains its usefulness. But once it's been splattered across the floor, once the thirsty earth has sucked it down, it's gone. Finished. Used up. Past reclamation.

"The Little Mermaid" is about *kenosis*. You won't get that from the Disney version, of course. To experience the full pathos of this story, the "terrible beauty" as William Butler Yeats might say, of its portrait of self-emptying sacrifice, you'll have to shut off the VCR, go to the library or a good used-book store, and find yourself a copy of Hans Christian Andersen's *Fairy Tales*. Unedited. But be forewarned: If you're not familiar with the story in its original form, you're in for a surprise.

The drama begins when the Little Mermaid, like so many other fairy-tale heroes and heroines, sets out to achieve a quest. Her challenge? To rise above the waves, become human, marry the handsome prince with whose sculptured likeness she has fallen in love—and so win for herself an immortal soul. What sets her apart from those other heroes and heroines is that she fails in this quest. Her hopes are dashed. But that's all just a prelude to the real story.

The climax comes when all has been lost. Her beloved prince has overlooked her and married another. The royal wedding bells have sealed her fate. Soon the sun will rise, her heart will break, and she will be reduced to foam on the surface of the sea. She understands this; it's all part of the bargain she struck with the sea-witch. The Little Mermaid's cup is tottering toward irrecoverable loss and irreversible doom.

It's at this point that she's given an unexpected second chance. Take the knife! Kill the prince! You can't have him anyway; why not save yourself? Set the cup aright before it's too late. Hold on to the last little bit of wine that still remains at the bottom. Plunge the blade into his heart and return to your life in the sea!

It all comes down to this one horrific moment of decision. In that split second she wavers, hesitates…then turns. She turns, her hand restrained by the power of love. Constrained by love, she hurls the knife far out over the waves, refusing to purchase her life at the cost of his. She inverts the cup, shakes out the last few drops…and vanishes in the early sunlight. That's *kenosis*.

Sound familiar? It should. We've heard this story many times before:

> Have this attitude in yourselves which was also in Christ Jesus, who, although He existed in the form of God, did not regard equality with God a thing to be grasped, but emptied Himself, taking the form of a bond-servant, and being made in the likeness of men. And being found in appearance as a man, He humbled Himself by becoming obedient to the point of death, even death on a cross. (Philippians 2:5-8, NASB)

The trial that confronted the Little Mermaid as she stood trembling over the sleeping couple with the glittering blade in her hand is the one that Jesus faced at almost every major turn in His earthly career. He, too, contended with the voice that whispers, "Forget the rest of them. Look out for Number One. If you don't, nobody else will."

He heard that voice in the wilderness, when the devil said, "All this authority I will give You" (Luke 4:6). He grappled with the same temptation when He prayed in Gethsemane: "Abba, Father, all things are possible for You. Take this cup away from Me!" (Mark 14:36). His enemies taunted Him with it even as He hung upon the cross: "He saved others; Himself He cannot save.

If He is the King of Israel, let Him now come down from the cross, and we will believe Him!" (Matthew 27:42).

He could have done it. At any moment, He might have called down twelve legions of angels to blast them all off the face of the earth. He could have stepped down from the cross and stood towering above the crowd, fearsome and splendid in the fullness of His glory, His eyes like flames, a crown of stars replacing the thorns upon His head, a bright two-edged sword proceeding out of His mouth. The knife lay at his fingertips, but He did not consider it "a thing to be grasped." Instead, he flung it far away and spilled the cup of His lifeblood over the ground in an act of complete and utterly self-abnegating love.

That's the story of the Little Mermaid. It's also the story of the Savior who not only laid down His life for His friends (John 15:13), but left His followers an example that they might do the same. As the apostle Paul wrote to his friends in Philippi:

> Yes, and if I am being poured out as a drink offering
> on the sacrifice and service of your faith, I am glad and
> rejoice with you all. For the same reason you also be glad
> and rejoice with me. (Philippians 2:17)

# Kɪss ᴏғ Lɪғᴇ

## *Death Is Not the End of the Story*

"Snow White and the Seven Dwarfs"
from the Brothers Grimm

*It was not long before she opened her eyes,
sat up, and was alive again.*

Rain thudded dully into the thatch of the cottage roof. Beyond the windows, blackness shrouded the trees of the surrounding forest. Inside, seven little men sat drooping before the fire, caps in hand, eyes fixed upon the floor.

She was dead. Snow White...the beautiful young maiden ...the light in their darkness. In spite of all the warnings, in spite of all the precautions they'd taken to protect her, she had let the old woman into the house. She had eaten the poisoned apple. And now she was dead.

What a dreary night! How different from that other night— so long ago, it seemed!—when they had discovered her asleep, draped across their seven stumpy beds. "Oh, my! Oh, my!" they had exclaimed. "What a beautiful child!"

She was a refugee, she told them. She had stumbled upon their house while fleeing from her stepmother, the wicked queen. They received her gladly and treated her as the princess they knew her to be. In return, she cooked, cleaned, and kept house.

And such a housekeeper! She brought a woman's touch to the dingy little cottage. She made the place a home. Her mere presence in the room was like the breath of white apple blossoms on the spring breeze. They had grown to love her. But now she was dead.

She lay at the top of a mountain, in a glass coffin they had fashioned for her. Beautiful in death as in life—skin white as snow, lips red as blood, hair black as ebony. Every day they went to pay their respects. Every day they laid fresh flowers on the glass coffin. But what was the use? She was dead. Nothing could bring her back.

So they sat without speaking while the fire crackled and the rain drummed on.

At length a knock sounded at the cottage door. Up jumped the little men. They rushed to the windows and peered out, their suspicions roused. But no—it was not the witch. Instead, a tall and handsome young man stood on the doorstep, the hood of his cloak drawn up against the rain.

"Let me have the glass coffin on the mountaintop!" he begged when they let him inside. "My father is a king. I can pay whatever you ask. I have seen the beautiful princess who sleeps there, and I can't go on living without her!"

"She is dead," the dwarfs said sadly, turning their faces aside that he might not see their tears. "The casket is not for sale."

"Then give it to me as a gift!" the prince persisted. "I promise to honor and cherish her as long as I live!"

Bowed by the forceful gale of the young man's fervent appeals, they agreed at last to grant him his request.

Next morning the dragging, sagging troop set off through the dark forest and up the rocky mountain trail, the prince and his entourage following behind. At the top they paused while the prince ordered his servants to raise the glass coffin and bear it upon their shoulders. The men were moving to obey his command when, unexpectedly, he stopped them with an upraised hand. "Wait!" he said.

Slowly he moved toward the coffin. The dwarfs watched breathlessly as the young man, overcome at the sight of Snow White's loveliness, raised the lid and bent to plant a kiss upon her lips. In a moment he straightened up and stood gazing down at her.

Suddenly, a fair, long-fingered hand reached up from inside the casket and rested on its gilded edge. The dwarfs gasped. Could it be true? Was there really movement within the coffin? In the next moment, the princess sat up, blinked, and looked around.

"Where am I?" she said.

The rain ceased. The sun flashed out from behind a cloud. The prince, beaming, bent down and embraced the radiant young girl.

And the little men? They capered and danced for pure joy.

❧

A good storyteller works hard to draw the various threads of his or her narrative together in a single preclimactic "black moment" of apparent hopelessness, the fabled darkness before the dawn. This is just another way in which imaginative story-craft reflects the reality of human life.

Have you ever found yourself in that place of utter despair? At that dead end where you realize there's no way forward and no way back? If so, you've had a preliminary encounter with that formidable foe the Bible calls "the last enemy" (1 Corinthians 15:26). You've had a foretaste of death.

Death. It's not just the termination of biological functions. It has a spiritual significance as deep as time itself. It's the end of the line. It's absolute darkness—the tangible, tactile kind that miners and spelunkers know when their light flickers out three hundred feet below the surface of the earth. A can't-see-your-hand-in-front-of-your-face sort of blackness without the faintest hint of a glimmer at the end of the tunnel.

That's what it was like for the seven little men who lived in the forest cottage beyond the seven hills when they came home from work and found the light of their world lying lifeless on the floor. Before Snow White, they had never really loved anybody. For years without number they had lived the barbaric and carefree life of confirmed bachelors. But then she came—white as snow, red as blood, black as ebony. And for them, her coming had been like a sudden awakening.

What were they feeling when they laid the beautiful maiden in a glass box and set her on top of a mountain? It's not hard to imagine. Just think of Frodo and Sam as they stood outside the eastern gate of Moria, trying to grasp the fact that Gandalf, their mentor, guide, and friend, had fallen into darkness. Picture Mary Magdalene weeping outside the open tomb. Think of the family members and friends of the thousands who died in the destruction of the twin towers of the World Trade Center. Remember how *you* felt when someone close to you suddenly and inexplicably vanished out of this life, leaving a vacuum in your existence.

Isn't it odd? No matter how often the philosophers, anthropologists, and biologists try to tell us that death is just a part of life, somehow the human heart refuses to buy it. Man, though doomed like the animals to die, finds it extremely difficult to accept death as his just and rightful portion. Unlike the beasts, he understands, fears, and resents his mortality. Try as he might, he can't get rid of a nagging suspicion that death, at any time and under any circumstances, is an unfair and unnatural intrusion. How can it be that this sparkling stream of conscious thought and feeling that we call *ourselves*—this flow of loyalty and love, hatred and anger, fear and delight, sorrow and joy—should simply cease? It's unthinkable. It's obscene. It boggles the mind and sets it reeling.

> But man dies and is laid away;
> Indeed, he breathes his last
> And where is he?…
> So man lies down and does not rise.
> Till the heavens are no more,
> They will not awake
> Nor be roused from their sleep.…
> If a man dies, shall he live again?
>            (Job 14:10,12,14)

Is it any wonder that resurrection, for all its natural, scientific, and philosophical implausibility, remains one of the most stubbornly held and deeply cherished of all human hopes and dreams? It's not just the desire to live, strong as that is within us, that fuels this flame. It's the longing to be reunited with the people who make our lives complete. It's the wish for genuine and lasting community—the one wish strong and nimble enough to overleap the grave.

What if it came true? What if that person you ache to see again suddenly stood before you? What if you could hear once more the reassuring note of his voice or feel the touch of her hand upon your arm?

The Bible contains a number of stories about people who experienced this very thing. The widow of Nain, for instance, whose only son, at a touch from Jesus, sat straight up on the bier, bringing the funeral procession to a rude and abrupt end (Luke 7:11-17). Or Jairus, the synagogue manager, whose little daughter opened her eyes and woke from death the instant He took her by the hand (Luke 8:54). Or the sisters Mary and Martha, whose brother, Lazarus, got up and walked out of the tomb in response to the Master's command (John 11:43-44).

Think for a moment about the implications of these incidents. Raised to life! Here again is that principle of reversal or turnaround that represents the very essence of the gospel message. This is the giddy and impossible promise that has been given to all who put their faith in Christ. If true, it changes everything.

I am the resurrection and the life. He who believes in Me, though he may die, he shall live. And whoever lives and believes in Me shall never die. (John 11:25-26)

The hour is coming, and now is, when the dead will hear the voice of the Son of God; and those who hear will live. (John 5:25)

Resurrection. A new beginning. The confidence that the dead end is not a dead end after all; that, ultimately, the black hole cannot swallow you up; that hopelessness will be turned on its ear at last; that you will see her or him again. This is the word of reassurance we all long to hear.

The story of "Snow White and the Seven Dwarfs" bears witness to this primal desire of the human heart. And the greatest Story of all, the Story that has burst into the world from beyond its outer rim—the tale of the God who entered history, became a man, and walked among us—declares that it can and will be fulfilled. For the same Jesus who "suffered under Pontius Pilate, was crucified, dead, and buried" is Himself "the firstfruits of those who have fallen asleep" (1 Corinthians 15:20). As Christians have reminded each other every Easter Sunday for the past two millennia, "He is risen! He is risen indeed!" At the touch of His kiss, we too, like the princess in the glass coffin, shall stir, sit up, and rise.

Awake, you who sleep,
Arise from the dead,
And Christ will give you light! (Ephesians 5:14)

# The Great Riddle

*Unlocking the Meaning of the Heart's Desire*

"The Golden Key" from the Brothers Grimm

*How could anybody be so silly as make a key*
*for which there was no lock?*

—GEORGE MacDONALD, "THE GOLDEN KEY"

Winter. A day of darkness, cold, and snow. Curtains, blankets, pillows, and billows of snow.

*Scrip, scrap, scrape!* Slowly, inch by inch, the rough nail-studded door of the little wooden hut forced its way open. If you had been there, you would have seen it plowing back the powdery snow that had drifted up so deeply against it, moving as if under its own power. And you might have jumped with surprise to see a hand suddenly shoot out from behind the door, then a foot, and a head—the curly black head of a boy about seven or eight years old.

The boy pushed his way through the narrow opening, pulled a shapeless woolen cap down over his ears, and stood blowing on his mittened hands. Then, seizing by its rope handle a wooden sled that leaned against the side of the house, he yanked it to the ground and dragged it across the yard, trudging heavily through the deep drifts. When he reached the gate, which rose no more than a foot or two above the surface of the snow, he climbed over, drew the sled after him, and headed for the woods.

It was his job to gather fuel for the fire. If he didn't, his mother and father and brothers and sisters would freeze. This was the harshest winter their poor family had ever known. So they sent him to bring home the wood. A simple task. But though he worked hard and fast, it took him most of the day to find enough twigs and branches to make a full load. Everything was covered in deep drifts of snow, and he had to dig for every bit of firewood he got.

At last it was time to turn for home, but he dared not set out without first building a fire to warm himself. Indeed, he had no choice. The only alternative would have been the loss of fingers and toes. Wolves, he knew, would soon be shadowing these woods. But at the moment, frostbite was the nearer and more threatening foe.

He got down on his knees and began to scoop the snow aside, clearing a space in which to pile his brush and kindling. He had nearly finished and was about to reach for a handful of twigs when something caught his eye. Something bright, shiny, and yellow glinted up at him from beneath the frozen soil. He brushed the last of the snow away from the bare earth and bent down for a closer look. It was a key! A shining golden key! He dug it out and held it up between his thumb and forefinger.

He stared at it in wonder. *Where there's a key,* he thought, *there must also be a lock.* That was just plain common sense.

And so, with fingers numbed by the cold, he began to dig again. Though unutterably weary, he scrabbled at the stone-hard, frostbitten earth, removing it grain by grain and pebble by pebble, until at last he touched something hard and unyielding—the lid of a little iron chest! His heart jumped into his throat. He forgot about his frozen fingers and worked with renewed zeal.

And now, as we watch him, he is lifting the chest out of the hole; he is brushing away the clinging clods of soil. Turning the precious thing over and over, he searches, searches, while the pulsing of his blood makes a thrumming noise in his ears.

No keyhole? How can it be? *Where there's a key, there must also be a lock.* But of course! He gasps with relief. His breath escapes into the dusky air in a feathery steam-white cloud. There *is* a hole! It was only caked over with a patch of clotted, frozen mud. Trembling with excitement, he knocks the mold away and tries the key. It fits!

And now he is turning the key in the lock…and now he is raising the lid of the chest on its squealing rusty hinges.

What wonderful things will he find inside?

Soon—very soon!—we'll know…

⚜

In the Russian tale of "The Enchanted Princess," a beautiful young czarevna is besieged by a houseful of suitors, each one eager to win her hand in marriage. She, however, like Penelope, the faithful wife of Odysseus, rebuffs them all. Why? Because she is convinced that the long-lost husband of her youth is destined to return; that he is, in fact, present in the house at that very moment, though invisible to the eye. So she presents a riddle to the horde of houseguests who have gathered in hopes of winning her heart:

> I had a home-made casket with a golden key; I lost this key, and did not think to find it: but now this key has found itself. Who guesses the riddle, him will I marry.[38]

The Golden Key is an image that recurs throughout fairy-tale literature, popping up now and again, here and there, in a number of different legends and in a variety of forms. The intriguing story fragment just retold falls near the end of the Grimms' collection. It's possible to argue that "The Golden Key," both by virtue of position and theme, makes a particularly fitting conclusion to the brothers' monumental contribution to the field of folklore and fantasy. The story's tantalizing lack of closure makes it an unforgettable example of that most alluring of all fairy enchantments: the end that is also a beginning.

What will the boy find when he opens the iron chest? That's a question with which to wile away many a long winter's evening. It's a question that has no sure and certain answer—which, of course, is exactly what makes it so deliciously irresistible, so mysteriously and mystically hopeful. Because we all have a feeling that, whatever he discovers, it must be something altogether marvelous. Something unimaginably precious and thoroughly life-changing.

But this, surprisingly enough, is not the most important thing about the Golden Key. The most important thing about it is also the most obvious—namely, that it is what it is: a key. A solitary, isolated key. Herein lies a mystery as big as the world itself. For as our young hero so perceptively discerns, *Where there's a key, there must also be a lock.* The one implies the existence of the other. Necessarily.

The tale of "The Golden Key" is the story of every human life. Yours and mine. A key by itself, lost and alone, lying loose upon the frozen ground—could there be a more poignant image of the human desire for context, meaning, and fulfillment? Somewhere this key must fit! It was made for a purpose; it cannot exist unto itself. In the language of the novelist and dramatist, the finding of the solitary key is an *inciting incident*. It instigates a search. It sparks the undertaking of a quest.

"But where was the lock to which the key belonged?" asks Mossy, protagonist of George MacDonald's creative twist and expansion on the Grimms' story. "It must be somewhere, for how could anybody be so silly as make a key for which there was no lock?"

Mossy is right. It would be silly to make a key without a lock. Just as it is silly to presume that there is nothing in the universe that corresponds to our innate longing for significance, our hunger for a relationship that will lift us above the level of the beasts and inanimate objects. No "Thou" to answer to the human "I."

Man alone among the creatures of the world is conscious of himself as a personal being. Though fragile and fleshly, he is nevertheless capable of contemplating his own frailty and mortality and recognizing his need of a transcendent Other. He is, as Blaise Pascal liked to call him, a "thinking reed."[39] This fact constitutes a riddle—a riddle that bears within itself the clue to its own solution. It's a key that implies the existence of a lock.

How in a trillion years could a roiling stew of impersonal matter have produced such a creature? What combination of amino acids could possibly have given rise to this nagging hope of finding a place "somewhere over the rainbow" where you and I can fit in? This is the question that no evolutionary theory, however thorough and consistent with the evidence, will ever be able to answer. As C. S. Lewis put it,

Creatures are not born with desires unless satisfaction for those desires exists. A baby feels hunger: well, there is such a thing as food. A duckling wants to swim: well, there is such a thing as water. Men feel sexual desire: well, there is such a thing as sex. If I find in myself a desire which no experience in this world can satisfy, the most probable explanation is that I was made for another world.[40]

Where there's a key, there must also be a lock. And where there are deep personal aspirations after something "no experience in this world can satisfy," there must also be a personal God who stands ready to fill that aching gap in the human soul.

God Himself is the lock for which the key was made. This is the resolution, the closure, the final answer for which every man and woman longs with his or her entire being. To know Him, to experience Him, to be filled with the power of His Spirit and the overflowing sweetness of His love—this is the goal we seek whether we know it or not.

The Russian tale of "The Enchanted Princess" reaches its climax when the frustrated suitors finally give up their attempts to solve the riddle. Then the princess turns and speaks, as it were, to the thin air:

"Show thyself, dear friend," she said.

The soldier removed his cap of invisibility, took her by the white hand, and began to kiss her on the sweet mouth.

"Here is the riddle for you," said the fair princess: "I am the home-made casket, and the golden key is my faithful husband."[41]

Our story will end in much the same way. The Bridegroom will come—"He who has the key of David, He who opens and no one shuts, and shuts and no one opens" (Revelation 3:7). He will take us by the hand and lead us to the door of His kingdom.

> My beloved put his hand
> By the latch of the door,
> And my heart yearned for him.
> I arose to open for my beloved,
> And my hands dripped with myrrh,
> My fingers with liquid myrrh,
> On the handles of the lock. (Song of Solomon 5:4-5)

Then the key will turn in the lock. The gates will swing open. And we, like the boy in the tale of "The Golden Key," will look upon treasures untold.

# Green Isle of the West

## Our Destiny Beyond This World

### "The Tale of Oisin and Niam" from Irish folklore

*Nor pain nor sickness knows the dweller there,*
*Death and decay come near him never more.*

Fionn MacCumhail, chief of the Fianna of Ireland, and Oisin his son, bard of Erin, went hunting with their men by the shores of Loch Lena. Around them hung the morning mists in a veil of golden haze. At their feet stretched the loch, its surface a sheet of beaten copper. Behind them burned the rising sun, a vague and shimmering pool of brightness in a cloud of swirling light.

Peering ahead in search of game, Fionn perceived a rolling eddy in the fog. As he watched, the eddy resolved into a shadow and the shadow congealed into a shape. Then the shape began to move purposefully toward them, rising as it were from the waters of the loch itself.

Gripping his spear, bright-eyed Fionn, chieftain among chieftains, stepped forward into the mists. Behind him clashed and clattered the weapons of his men as they came crowding after him. Beside him loped the two hounds, Bran and Sceolan. How he marveled to see the strange demeanor of the dogs! For they neither barked, growled, nor howled at the intruder, but lay down with their black snouts between their paws, a meek and submissive expression in their dark brown eyes.

Looking up, Fionn beheld a wonder. Before him stood a tall, snow-white steed and seated on it a beautiful and stately maiden, dressed as a queen. A dark brown mantle of silk, set with stars of red gold, draped her lovely form in rich folds and trailed generously upon the ground. Upon her head rested a crown of gleaming gold.

Bold Fionn groped for words. He found none. He tried to move, but his feet were fixed fast to the damp earth. Deep silence, thicker than the mists, descended upon the gathered warriors of the Fianna. Out of the corner of his eye the chieftain saw the face of his son, pale as if with the sickness of a great desire.

The maiden drew near. "Know you whence I come?" she asked. "I have traveled far, and now at last I have found you, Fionn son of Cumhail."

The hero shifted awkwardly and pulled at his beard. He grunted. Again he caught sight of Oisin's face, lips parted, the light of a distant flame glittering in his eyes. "Forgive me, maiden," said Fionn at last, "but I do not know your name."

"I am Niam of the Golden Hair," she answered, "daughter of the King of the Land of Youth, which is in the Green Isle of the West. It is love for your son Oisin that brings me here."

Before Fionn could put out a hand to stop him, Oisin stepped forward out of the ranks. Step by step he moved toward her, as if in a dream. She turned and spoke to the young man in a voice as clear as her piercing blue-green eyes.

"Will you come with me, Oisin, to my father's land?

Delightful is the land beyond all dreams,
Fairer than aught thine eyes have ever seen.
There all the year the fruit is on the tree,
And all the year the bloom is on the flower.[42]

Oisin never faltered. "I *will* go," he said firmly, his cheeks aflame with a keen and eager hope. And as he said it, Fionn and every other man present knew beyond doubt that he would have given the same answer in the young bard's place.

Then, as the strains of the maiden's song still hung in the air, Oisin mounted the fairy steed and clasped her in his arms. Fionn and his men stood watching, hardly daring to breathe, as Niam of the Golden Hair reined her horse about and gave the bridle a ringing shake. Then off she flew with the chieftain's son, into the dispersing mists, down the glade, and away over the shining waters of the loch.

It was the last time any of them saw Oisin son of Fionn on earth.

⚜

Celtic lore tells of a verdant spot beyond the boundaries of this world, a place where time is not, where joys never end, and where youth, health, and abundant life fill every crack and cranny of the soul to overflowing. It is called the Green Isle of the West.

We end with a tale very much like that with which we began: a tale in which a person from that Green Isle—that Wood Beyond the World, that Well at the World's End—emerges out of the eternal mist and calls a bewildered mortal to come away to a land of heartbreaking beauty and everlasting life.

But though similar, the tale of Thomas the Rhymer and the story of Oisin and Niam are strikingly different in at least one important detail. Thomas undertakes his journey into Faerie against his will, as a hostage and a captive. The queen of Elfland abducts him, making him her indentured servant for seven years. And she does so at least partly in response to Thomas's own folly and naiveté.

Oisin, on the other hand—son of Ireland's greatest warrior and chief of the Irish poets and bards—leaps wholeheartedly into the saddle behind Niam and accompanies her to her father's land without once looking back. Eagerly he responds to the call of his other-worldly wooer, for his heart and mind are captured entirely by the vision she sets before him: a vision of a place where death and disease are no more, where sorrow is forgotten, and where unending youth is the lot of the blessed inhabitants. With his eyes fixed upon that goal, Oisin forsakes his father, leaves his friends behind, and ventures into the shining west with the golden-haired girl.

Who can blame him? Who wouldn't do the same if given the chance?

> Oh, sisters, can't you hear it,
> And don't you want to go
> And leave this world of trial
> And trouble here below?[43]

The elves of J. R. R. Tolkien's Middle-earth know a similar longing. Tolkien's "Green Isle" is Tol Eressea, the Lonely Island, situated in the Bay of Eldamar or Elvenhome, original abode of the elves in the deathless lands of the West.[44] Even as the epic trilogy of *The Lord of the Rings* begins, elvish folk are leaving Middle-earth in droves, going down to the Grey Havens to board the swan-prowed white ships and sail away forever, away to the land of their heart's desire, to the place where they have always belonged. The Lady Galadriel warns Legolas, a wood elf who has spent his entire life in the forest, that he will not be able to resist the draw of this passionate desire if once he catches sight of the Sundering Seas:

> Legolas Greenleaf, long under tree,
> In joy thou hast lived. Beware of the Sea!
> If thou hearest the cry of the gull on the shore,
> Thy heart shall then rest in the forest no more.[45]

There *is* a Green Isle in the West. We were made for it, and as in the case of Legolas and Oisin son of Fionn, it beckons to us, wooing our hearts to draw near. It is, in some sense, the place of our original abode, the paradise where God placed the man and the woman on that bright and distant morning when He first created them:

> The LORD God planted a garden eastward in Eden, and there He put the man whom He had formed. And out of the ground the LORD God made every tree grow that is pleasant to the sight and good for food. The tree of life was also in the midst of the garden, and the tree of the knowledge of good and evil. (Genesis 2:8-9)

Ever since Adam and Eve were driven out of Eden, their children and heirs have been wishing and hoping, working and striving, pouring their hearts into an effort to find a way back to the garden. Somewhere, they are sure, there *must* be a homeland more perfectly suited to their longings and conformed to the inner landscape of their souls. Indeed, they half remember it in dreams...and in the stories they tell.

> I found myself at the window, whose gloomy curtains
> were withdrawn, and where I stood gazing on a whole
> heaven of stars, small and sparkling in the moonlight.
> Below lay a sea, still as death and hoary in the moon,
> sweeping into bays and around capes and islands, away,
> away, I knew not whither. Alas! it was no sea, but a low
> fog burnished by the moon. "Surely there is such a sea
> somewhere!" said I to myself.[46]

There *is* such a sea and beyond it a land that corresponds in every detail to our fading recollections of the country we left behind so long ago. The ancient Scots and Irish called it the Green Isle of the West, the Land of Perpetual Youth. Christians call it heaven. And though, since the shape of the world was changed, it has slipped below the horizon of human sight, we can and will reach it if, like Oisin son of Fionn, we will only respond to the call of the One who has come forth from that isle and invited us to return with Him. That land is our final destination, our lasting home. It is a country of unending joys and delights, devoid of all sorrow and suffering, more wondrous by far than anything the human eye has seen or the human mind conceived.

It is the New Jerusalem which, according to the promise of Scripture, is to come down out of heaven as a bride adorned for her husband:

> And he showed me a pure river of water of life, clear as crystal, proceeding from the throne of God and of the Lamb. In the middle of its street, and on either side of the river, was the tree of life, which bore twelve fruits, each tree yielding its fruit every month. The leaves of the tree were for the healing of the nations. And there shall be no more curse, but the throne of God and of the Lamb shall be in it, and His servants shall serve Him. They shall see His face, and His name shall be on their foreheads. There shall be no night there: They need no lamp nor light of the sun, for the Lord God gives them light. And they shall reign forever and ever. (Revelation 22:1-5)

Heaven. Paradise regained. Nothing short of this awaits those who hear the call and answer: "Rise up, my love, my fair one, and come away. For lo, the winter is past, the rain is over and gone" (Song of Solomon 2:10-11).

# Epilogue

# EYES TO SEE

## *"Second Sight"*

*The lamp of the body is the eye.*
*If therefore your eye is good,*
*your whole body will be full of light.*

—MATTHEW 6:22

A tale is told in Scotland of a woman who was gifted with the fabled "second sight"—the ability to see spiritual realities and the invisible truths of the Other World. This rare and highly coveted gift was bestowed upon her in exchange for a favor she'd granted to the fairies, willingly and graciously enough, though not entirely as a volunteer. It seems that on a certain evening a strange woman, clad all in green, had appeared on her doorstep with a beautiful child on her arm.

"Will you nurse my bonnie baby until I return?" asked the fairy (for such indeed she was).

The woman stared for a moment, completely at a loss. Then she heard her own voice saying, "Yes. Certainly I'll do that."

A year passed. During all that time, the woman never lacked for food, fuel, or clothing; all the material and physical needs of her household were miraculously and abundantly supplied. At last the fairy returned.

"You have been kind to my bonnie baby," said she. "Come with me, and I shall show you my house."

The woman followed her through a shaded wood and up a sunny green hillside. Near the top of the hill the fairy lifted up a turf in the bank, revealing a wooden door. She opened the door, and the two of them entered.

"What do you see?" asked the lady in green.

The woman squinted in the dim light. "Not much," she said. "A bare chamber. A dirt floor."

From her waist belt the fairy drew forth a goblet containing a green liquid. She poured three drops into the woman's left eye.

"Now," she said, "you shall see my home. Look again!"

The woman did. And as she looked, she was filled with wonder. Before her lay a spacious and beautiful country; away and away it stretched into the dim blue distance. There were green hills fringed by trees, crystal streams flashing in the bright daylight, and a lake that shone like burnished silver. Between the hills a field of ripe barley shone golden and rippling in the sun.

For many years afterward the woman retained this capacity to see what others were entirely unable to discern.

Only the fairies could have given her such a gift. Only the fairies could take it away.[47]

❦

This story presents, in parable form, a neat little picture of what we have been attempting to do in this book. We've been looking for God in fairy tales—seeking eternal truth in places where many sane and sensible people would say it simply can't be found.

We have climbed the hill, lifted the turf, opened the wooden door, and stepped inside. Now it's time to ask ourselves what we've seen. Was it simply a bare earthen chamber? Or have we instead found ourselves gazing out over an expansive, golden country bathed in everlasting light? In an important sense, it all depends upon the power of perception residing within the individual eye.

Truth, beauty, and goodness. Our efforts to examine fantasy, folk tales, and fairy stories through Christ-colored glasses have given us all three in rich abundance. But the surprising thing is that they have also yielded something more—something rare, precious, and altogether unexpected. For those who have eyes to see, this journey ends with a vision every bit as radical as the gospel itself.

A radical vision. That, in the final analysis, is perhaps the most striking aspect of the discoveries we've made along the road to Fairy Land. If there is any "religion" at all to be found in the world of Hansel and Gretel, Peter Pan, Mary Poppins, Snow White, and the Little Mermaid, it is most certainly not the religion of comfortable complacency, Pharisaic law keeping, and moralistic do-goodery. It's more in the nature of a shocking slap in the face. A blast of cold air through an open door. A stinging draught of a bitter but healing potion.

In the past, it's been fairly common to use the fairy tales as a basis for moralizing—as raw material from which to draw wise maxims, prudent precepts, and helpful tips for living. Charles Perrault indulged a penchant for this kind of thing in the 1697 edition of his *Histoires ou contes du temps passé*. Here, in verse form, is the lesson he appends to the tale of Cinderella:

> Godmothers are useful things
> Even when without the wings.
> Wisdom may be yours and wit,
> Courage, industry, and grit—
> What's the use of these at all,
> If you lack a friend at call?[48]

A pleasant sentiment, to be sure. A comforting, inspirational thought. Still, it's pretty bland, innocuous stuff. Definitely not the kind of gold one expects to find in a mother-lode mine. And as we've seen, a story like "Cinderella," when viewed through the eyes of Christian faith, has something quite different to offer. Something far more astringent and disturbing. Something downright shocking and revolutionary. At its heart, the tale of "Cinderella" is the story of the mustard seed and the treasure hidden in the field. It's the tale of the poor and the lame, the sick and the blind, the prostitutes and sinners and tax collectors who go dancing into the kingdom ahead of the rich and the righteous. It's a reversal, a turnaround, an upset—a disastrous eucatastrophe. It's reminiscent of the tale of the boy who felled a giant with a sling and a stone. Or the baby in the manger who shook Caesar's mighty empire.

That's why "Cinderella" and "The Little Mermaid" and "The Wild Swans" and "The Bremen Town Musicians," when viewed through Christ-colored glasses, have such an authentic aura of the gospel about them. They're not just nice little nursery tales. In them lie hidden the painful, heartrending, hope-giving seeds of upheaval, controversy, and metamorphosis: whispers and rumors of a coming change that promises to turn the whole world on its ear.

In this way, these tales are remarkably like the stories Jesus told. For Jesus never engaged in mere moralizing. He hadn't the slightest interest in turning His listeners into nicer people or more productive citizens. His parables were never intended to inspire anyone to greater thrift, industry, responsibility, or patriotism. Instead, they take us by the throat, turn us on our heads, and rattle us to the core. They challenge us to lay aside preconceived notions, to abandon prejudice and presumption. They do this by arresting our attention with a vision of a kingdom so outlandishly marvelous and crazy, so radically different from anything we could ever have conceived or invented in our own power, that it's nearly impossible to wrap the human mind around it.

Jesus invites us to follow Him into that topsy-turvy kingdom, where, like Alice through the Looking-glass, we encounter inversion, conversion, paradox, and surprise at almost every turn in the road. Trembling on the borders of that strange land, we, like Dorothy, can only stare in wide-eyed wonder and say, "Toto, I have a feeling we're not in Kansas anymore."

Why? Because this kingdom is a place where the first are last, the poor are rich, and the weak are strong. Where children and beggars are kings and lords, and death and failure the paths to victory and life. Where to lose one's life is to save it, and all the power, prestige, and prominence the world has to offer are worth no more than a pile of dung. Where fear is wisdom and contentment is wealth. Where "what is highly esteemed among men is an abomination in the sight of God" (Luke 16:15).

A world turned upside-down and inside-out—*that* is what so many of the fairy tales reveal in one way or another. And that is what Jesus offers to those who have eyes to see, ears to hear, and hearts to receive the vision.

# Notes

1. As quoted in Humphrey Carpenter, *Tolkien: A Biography* (New York: Ballantine Books, 1977), 163-5. The conversation between Tolkien and Lewis presented here is a fictionalized retelling of an incident cited in Carpenter's work.

2. G. K. Chesterton, *The Everlasting Man* (New York: Image Books, 1955), 111.

3. Chesterton, *The Everlasting Man*, 103, 251.

4. Maurice Sendak, *Higglety Pigglety Pop! or There Must Be More to Life* (New York: Harper and Row, 1967), 5.

5. Augustine, *Confessions*, as quoted in *Great Books of the Western World* vol. 18, bk. 1 (Chicago: Encyclopedia Britannica, 1952), 1.

6. C. S. Lewis, *The Last Battle* (New York: Collier, 1956), 161.

7. J. R. R. Tolkien, "Tree and Leaf," *The Tolkien Reader* (New York: Ballantine Books, 1966), 72.

8. As quoted in Hans Christian Andersen, *Hans Andersen's Fairy Tales*, trans. L. W. Kingsland (Oxford: Oxford University Press, 1984), ix.

9. Naomi Lewis, introduction to *Hans Andersen's Fairy Tales*, ix.

10. C. S. Lewis, *God in the Dock* (Grand Rapids: Eerdmans, 1970), 66-7.

11. Tolkien, *The Tolkien Reader*, 71-2.

12. Chesterton, *The Everlasting Man*, 115.

13. Sir Walter Scott, *The Lady of the Lake and Other Poems* (New York: New American Library, 1962), 304.

14. Scott, *Lady of the Lake.*

15. Scott, *Lady of the Lake,* 305.

16. Francis Thompson, "The Kingdom of God: 'In No Strange Land,'" in *Complete Poetical Works of Francis Thompson* (New York: Boni and Liveright, 1918), 357.

17. C. S. Lewis, *The Magician's Nephew* (New York: Collier, 1955), 28-40.

18. Tolkien, *The Tolkien Reader,* 33.

19. Paul Brand and Philip Yancey, *In His Image* (Grand Rapids: Zondervan, 1984), 235.

20. P. L. Travers, *Mary Poppins* (New York: Dell, 1981), 11-2.

21. C. S. Lewis, *Reflections on the Psalms* (San Diego: Harcourt Brace Jovanovich, 1958), 119.

22. Andersen, *Hans Andersen's Fairy Tales,* 233, 271.

23. Thompson, "The Hound of Heaven," in *Complete Poetical Works of Francis Thompson,* 88.

24. Thompson, "The Hound of Heaven," 93.

25. "And Can It Be That I Should Gain?" words by Charles Wesley, 1738.

26. Joseph Jacobs, comp., "Jack the Giant-Killer," in *English Fairy Tales* (New York: Dover, 1967), 101.

27. Tolkien, *The Tolkien Reader,* 60.

28. Jacobs, "Jack the Giant-Killer," 99.

29. Peter Christen Asbjørnsen and Jørgen Moe, "Princess on the Glass Hill," in *East o' the Sun and West o' the Moon,* trans. George Webbe Dasent (New York: Dover, 1970), 103.

30. Jack Zipes, trans., "Cinderella," in *The Complete Fairy Tales of the Brothers Grimm,* vol. 1, *Tales 1-100* (New York: Bantam Books, 1987), 84.

31. "Sweet Little Jesus Boy," traditional spiritual.

32. William Wordsworth, "Ode: Intimations of Immortality from Recollections of Early Childhood," in *William Wordsworth: Selected Poems* (New York: Gramercy Books, 1993), 135.

33. Jackie Wullschläger, *Inventing Wonderland: The Lives and Fantasies of Lewis Carroll, Edward Lear, J. M. Barrie, Kenneth Grahame and A. A. Milne* (New York: The Free Press, 1995), 27.

34. Chesterton, *The Everlasting Man,* 203.

35. J. M. Barrie, *Peter Pan* (originally *Peter Pan and Wendy*) (New York: Bantam Skylark, 1982), 179.

36. Vernard Eller, *The Outward Bound: Caravaning as the Style of the Church* (Grand Rapids: Eerdmans, 1980), 12.

37. Andersen, *Hans Andersen's Fairy Tales,* 161.

38. Jeremiah Curtin, *Myths and Folk-tales of the Russians, Western Slavs, and Magyars* (Mineola, N. Y.: Dover Publications, 1999), 247-8.

39. Blaise Pascal, *Pensées,* trans. A. J. Krailsheimer (New York: Penguin Books, 1966) #200 (347), 95.

40. C. S. Lewis, *Mere Christianity* (New York: Simon & Schuster, 1996), 121.

41. Curtin, *Myths and Folk-tales,* 248.

42. T. W. Rolleston, *Celtic Myths and Legends* (New York: Dover, 1990), 271.

43. "Talk About Suffering," traditional; as sung by Doc Watson, Vanguard Records, © 1985, 1987.

44. J. R. R. Tolkien, *The Silmarillion* (Boston: Houghton Mifflin, 1977), 57ff.

45.   J. R. R. Tolkien, *The Lord of the Rings* (Boston: Houghton Mifflin, 1955, 1965, 1983), 524.

46.   George MacDonald, *Phantastes and Lilith* (Grand Rapids: Eerdmans, 1964), 18.

47.   Donald A. Mackenzie, "A Vision of the Dead," in *Scottish Wonder Tales from Myth and Legend* (Mineola, N.Y.: Dover, 1997), 122-5.

48.   Charles Perrault, *Perrault's Fairy Tales,* trans. A. E. Johnson (New York: Dover, 1969), 77-8.